ANYTHING GOES!

LARRY KING

WITH PAT PIPER

ANYTHING
GOES!

What I've Learned from Pundits, Politicians, and Presidents

WARNER BOOKS

A Time Warner Company

Copyright © 2000 by Larry King
All rights reserved.

Warner Books, Inc., 1271 Avenue of the Americas, New York, NY 10020

Visit our Web site at www.twbookmark.com

W A Time Warner Company

Printed in the United States of America

First Printing: November 2000

10 9 8 7 6 5 4 3 2 1

Library of Congress Cataloging-in-Publication Data
King, Larry, 1933-
    Anything goes! : what I've learned from pundits, politicians, and presidents /
Larry King with Pat Piper.
        p. cm.
    Includes index.
    ISBN 0-446-52528-6
    1. King, Larry, 1933- 2. Broadcasters—United States—Biography.
3. United States—Politics and government—20th century. I. Piper, Pat.
II. Title.

PN1991.4.K45 A3 2000
791.44'092—dc21
[B]   00-044931

To Chance, born in 1999, and Cannon, born in 2000.
I hope your years will not be a time where anything goes.

Acknowledgments

This two-year project is the result not only of these times, but these people:

Warner Books president, Larry Kirshbaum, and literary agent Ed Victor were on the same page long before the first word was written.

Warner editor Rick Wolff guided and framed these words despite these times where anything goes.

The staff of *Larry King Live* brought pundits, politicians, and presidents to your television every night.

And Ted Turner, whose vision twenty years ago of a cable news channel allows the world to see itself today.

Larry King   Pat Piper

Contents

Introduction

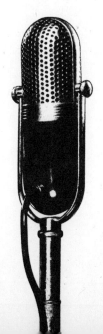

March 18, 1993. Washington, D.C. The Radio-Television Correspondents Dinner is in full swing at the Washington Hilton. It's an annual black-tie event where more than a thousand reporters, producers, editors, news writers, bookers, columnists, anchors, and (of course) talk show hosts gather for dinner with members of Congress, ambassadors, and the president of the United States. It is one of the few evenings of the year where absolutely no serious business is conducted other than establishing a working relationship with those in the offices at the networks and those in the offices the networks cover.

This was Bill Clinton's first formal dinner with the Washington media since winning the White House five months earlier, with 43 percent of the popular vote. He was the fourteenth president elected without a majority and, as if to prove the point, Senate Minority Leader Bob Dole announced less than twenty-four hours after the votes were counted that the GOP, and not Bill Clinton, represented the 57 percent who had voted either for George Bush or Ross Perot. I remember thinking to myself it's really true when they say the next election begins as soon as the current one ends. And I had one other thought about this fact: a single word, "unfortunately."

But when he was introduced at the dinner that evening, Clinton received an enthusiastic round of applause. I looked around the huge room, and that's when I noticed something else: Everyone rose to their feet. My take was the people in this room wanted the president to do well. It brought to mind a moment so many years earlier during my late-night radio show, when I had this very conversation with a caller. He was going on about how much he despised the newly elected George Bush, and I said to him, "Don't you want Bush to succeed, and don't you think if he succeeds then the country will succeed?" The caller said he didn't see it that way, and if George Bush does well that means the country goes to hell. While many have said what happens in Washington has nothing whatsoever to do with anything happening anywhere else in the country, I think what was occurring in that hotel ballroom was indeed a mirror of America in early 1993. Give the new guy a chance. Even Bob Dole stood during the introduction of the new president and applauded along with everyone else and I believed he wanted Clinton to do well, if only during this speech. And that evening Bill Clinton did well at the podium.

Never lose your sense of humor. And remember that
most of us who do this on both sides do it because
we love our country and prefer to believe that an

effort made today can make it better tomorrow. It's a good way to live a life.

It's a tough way to live a life is what I was thinking as he spoke. And getting to that point was just as tough. The 1992 presidential election had been an extraordinary time in America. Things occurred that proved pundit after pundit flat-out wrong. It left the candidates bruised, it brought in a wild card third party candidate who defied every expert with infomercials, money, and charts, and captured, if only for a while, America's imagination and ignited an expectation that we can do better. It brought defeat to an incumbent president who only a year earlier had a 90 percent approval rating. I knew the way we elect and watch and report on a president was going to be different from now on as a result of what had just happened. Talk about understatements.

But in this room on this night the only issue facing the president and the audience was accessibility. Bill Clinton hadn't had a news conference since being sworn in two months earlier. And already the pundits and analysts and "experts" were sitting on talk shows, including mine, saying he's gotta get out there, he'd better start facing the voters, he needs to sell his hundred-day agenda to the public (it was now Day 58 for those who insisted on counting) and blah blah blah. That's when I realized Bill Clinton was looking right at me.

You know why I can stiff you on press conferences? Because Larry King liberated me by giving me to the American people directly.

Everyone at the CNN tables chimed in with encouraging shouts of "all right, Larry!" and slaps on the back and applause, but let me tell you, the rest of the room turned cold real fast. I could feel the glare from everyone else on a single point on the back of my head, sort of like the red laser that falls on a person in video games or the movies before someone else pulls a trigger. So much for the advice about keeping a sense of humor.

After Clinton finished and while we were all standing and applauding, some yahoo I didn't know yelled from a few tables away, "Hey Larry, are you the teacher's pet?" I smiled and looked back toward the podium. And once again my mind was at work thinking how wonderful it is for a poor Jewish kid from Brooklyn to be recognized by the president of the United States while at the same time thinking how horrible it is that a poor Jewish kid from Brooklyn was recognized by the president of the United States. Bill Clinton had talked for about ten minutes and the entire room had only heard one line.

The room was still freezing when the dinner came to an end and I decided to just get the hell out of the Washington Hilton and walk to my car. The March air felt balmy compared to where I had been for the past three hours. And I realized something as I walked: Bill Clinton was right.

Something happened in 1992 that changed American politics. Instead of a president holding a prime-time news conference and being asked questions by the same people who always ask questions, the venue had changed. I know it wasn't the result of a bunch of media experts sitting around a table saying let's bypass Sam Donaldson and all the other White House correspondents and have our guy talk directly to the lady in Des Moines. Media experts aren't that smart. It was different now. Presidents, and candidates for president, all of whom are quick to tell you they represent the American people, could now answer questions directly from viewers or listeners and therefore circumvent the Washington correspondent filter altogether. It happened when Ross Perot had appeared on my show a year earlier and it happened when Bill Clinton took questions on *Good Morning America* or appeared on Arsenio Hall and played saxophone and when President Bush was a guest on *Today*. The medium was the message and the message was very clear: The disillusioned American could ask questions just as well, if not better, of a candidate as could the highly paid reporter. I think that was *the* story from the 1992 presidential election. All of us had been witness to a strategic shift in the way we approach a candidate and, just as important, in the way a candidate approaches us. And for many in the main ballroom at the Washington Hilton, the idea just made them sick.

As I drove home that evening I turned the radio to a favorite big band station just in time to hear the words "the world has gone mad today." It was Cole Porter's "Anything Goes."

That was it. In 1992, we learned what once was the norm is no more. Maybe it happens before every millennium? Maybe that's why Caesar got knocked off two thousand years earlier? Maybe it's the result of technology speeding up the world? Maybe it's just that the only constant in life is that nothing stays the same? Or maybe Cole Porter had just taught the rest of us something?

By the time I pulled into my condo parking lot the events of the past thirty minutes had made one thing crystal clear: 1992 had been an incredible year and we'll probably never go through another one like it and Bill Clinton must be glad, as am I, that things will finally slow down.

I guess you could call that the Understatement of the Millennium.

CHAPTER ONE

Bill
Who?

July 20, 1988. I'm sitting in a CNN booth overlooking the floor of the Omni Arena in Atlanta. A couple hundred feet below, five thousand Democrats were preparing to make Massachusetts governor Michael Dukakis their nominee for president of the United States. My television show, *Larry King Live*, had been preempted in order to carry the speeches, all of which were designed to rally the delegates on the floor, but more important, the national television audience, around the fact this "son of Greek immigrants," as he described himself again and again and again, was preferable to George Bush.

And, like most of the delegates, I wasn't paying much attention. Someone was speaking and speaking and speaking and as he did, I kept thinking how typically democratic this was because every person whom we never knew before and will never see again gets a chance to make their point, get their fifteen minutes of fame (although this guy at the podium was way past that point), and then disappear until the next convention. Democratic conventions are like a Cubs game; there is noise and ethnics. Democrats will tell you 8:45 and they may get around to it by 9:20. Republicans, on the other hand, have orchestrated and smooth-running get-togethers. They tell you 8:45 and it's 8:45. It's a bunch of starched shirts and ties. It's an Amway convention. I guess the difference between the two political parties goes like this: After the speeches at a GOP convention you can always meet for a drink. At a Democratic convention the speeches never end before last call.

"Who the hell is that guy?" someone asked.

"He's doing *Hamlet* I think," another said.

"I don't think so," came another answer. "Even Hamlet never went on this long."

I thought about where I had been the past hour. CNN decided to send me to the convention floor for "quick hits," short interviews with newsmakers, delegates, or celebrities who were just taking a stroll, if one can stroll with five thousand others and two thousand members of the media. It had been one of the most bizarre moments I'd ever experienced. At 8:30 I was scheduled to talk to Richard M. Daley, the mayor of Chicago and the son of Mayor Richard J. Daley, who, even after death, held the patent on the idea of machine politics. As I walked to my position I passed Chris Wallace of NBC and Sam Donaldson of ABC and Dan Scanlan of Mutual Radio, who were huddled around someone with name recognition. I remember thinking to myself how hungry they all looked in this Neverland where dogs eat dogs alive.

At 8:29:10 I'm standing with Mayor Daley waiting to go on the air and looking at two delegates next to me with huge plastic Swiss cheese hats on their heads. This is how we choose the person to serve in the most powerful office in the world. Then two people walk by handing out bags of their state almonds and state candy (and Ohio candy corn looks like the Iowa candy corn from my perspective. And while we're on the topic, an almond is an almond, so that whole thing is a sham). "Something," I said to myself, "is off here."

All the reporters wore these Mars-like antenna headsets with a producer yelling nonstop in their ears. I was amazed that CBS didn't get into my CNN headset, and I figured if they did, I'd do what I was told. But I didn't give anyone any grief, choosing, instead, to just listen for instructions on this maiden voyage into Wackoland. I was told to move closer to the Chicago mayor so we could be in a good camera position, to look in a certain direction, and to ask three questions and then throw it back to Bernie Shaw, who was anchoring in the booth next to where I was now sitting watching all of this. I talked to the mayor and handed off to Bernie. And then a producer said, "Larry, you're outta here. Good job." I walked away thinking my next contract with CNN will have a clause for combat pay.

Actually, many of those who wear the daily media credential on a chain around the neck (yellow is Tuesday, which goes well with a blue shirt, white was Wednesday, which works with stripes) dress the part. I think in the month before any political convention, Banana Republic sells out every khaki vest it makes. Everyone wears these things, pockets loaded with pens and notepads for recording history's bold moments or, as is the usual case, dinner arrangements (I didn't own one because my dinners were always at CNN). But the vests were everywhere. And the wearers wore a scowl, as if this assignment placed the burden of mankind on their

5

shoulders. Every time I walked into the Mutual Broadcasting System booth that week I would see three of them in front of a microphone. Made me think I was looking at the Yalta summit or, when they smiled, the Andrews Sisters.

I looked at the bank of television monitors to my side. He was *still talking*. CNN was, of course, carrying the speech. But both NBC and ABC had dumped out with one doing commentary and the other running some kind of documentary about the early years of the son of the Greek immigrants. I knew damn well that if I was getting restless, the folks watching at home were way beyond restless. It brought to mind a moment about a year earlier when the executive producer of *60 Minutes*, Don Hewitt, and I had been standing in the green room of *Larry King Live* before going on the air. Someone wanted to change the channel (away from CNN to a ballgame, if I remember correctly) and Hewitt said to me the most important invention of the twentieth century wasn't the cure for polio or the Wright brothers' flight or unleaded gasoline or talk shows. It was the remote control. And at that very moment, nobody could find the remote control. I changed the channel by hand just as an intern produced it from underneath a sofa across the room.

"You know that clicker?" Hewitt said, looking at me. "It's going to change the world more than any other thing."

For a moment, I thought about it. He was crazy.

"It sits as a force in your hand. You can change stations with a button. You change advertisers' income. You force networks to think about every fifteen minutes of programming now." Hewitt was looking right at me as I did the math: Network execs think four times during my show. This was news.

It was during a commercial break, and we were changing

guests, that I realized Hewitt may be on to something. Here we were shifting into a totally different topic after half an hour on the air. I was ready to keep going with the discussion, but then I'm the guy who spent an entire hour in Atlantic City interviewing Kool and the Gang just trying to figure out the reason for the band's name. I have no problem interviewing someone for an hour. Watching me interview someone for an hour, however, is a whole different matter. The audience has an "electronic restlessness," as *Washington Post* columnist Howard Kurtz once told me, so if they start getting bored with a person or a topic or a segment or a suspender color, the finger goes to the clicker—if it isn't already positioned on the clicker in the first place. That's why guests are on and then off and we move to the next topic. Even as early as 1988, we were beginning to eat everything in sight and spit it out while moving to the next food source. The truth is, I didn't get this at first.

Hewitt's theory stayed with me until a few days later, when I decided he wasn't crazy at all. The clicker is control. If I can't find it after the maid cleans my California house, all hell breaks loose. When I travel to my house in Virginia, I have to learn all the channel numbers all over again and that makes for some rough moments. I've learned we all want control in our life and I can say the happiest people I know are those who can generally control their environment. The clicker gives the bus driver control when he can't do anything about the weather or tell his wife what to do. But he can control what he watches and what occupies his time. That's one description about these times: Control is moving away from the outside and toward each of us. The clicker was the first step in that direction.

Speaking of which, nobody in the Omni could control

this guy at the podium, who was still going. I watched gestures from floor managers for him to get off the stage but they were ignored. Maybe, I thought to myself, this was another form of control? Maybe this guy had never before been the center of attention? I felt sorry for him, more so than for those at home watching him. Certainly, as I've said, nobody on the floor was paying any attention. Obviously, I reasoned, he must be a hard worker who delivered some key districts to Dukakis during the primaries in order to be given such a prominent platform this evening. And then I thought, "Keep your day job, pal."

That was the moment he said, "In closing . . ." The arena erupted in applause and the loudest cheers of the night echoed through the hall. Even the technicians and producers at CNN were yelling. I just shook my head as the name graphic appeared on the air monitor. This wasn't any ward committee man who had delivered votes doing the telethon. It was the governor of Arkansas: Bill Clinton.

Even before Clinton took the podium, one television-savvy person knew this was going to be a disaster. Bob Shrum had been a speechwriter for Ted Kennedy and was now a powerful political consultant for numerous congressional and presidential campaigns. He had been given a copy of the Clinton speech a few minutes earlier and could tell right away it was too long. Shrum tried to reach the Dukakis camp to warn them but realized there just wasn't time to make any changes and, even if there were a few extra minutes for rewrites, someone with the Massachusetts governor must have approved the speech.

Shrum was right. The Massachusetts governor did approve it. Michael Dukakis told me years later he thought it was a pretty good speech, but in glancing at the pages never realized how long it was going to run. He considered Bill Clinton a guy with a good sense of the audience and if he started to run long, a natural circuit breaker would kick in to telescope the words and thoughts he wanted to convey. Dukakis selected the Arkansas governor to give the nominating speech because he had worked with Bill Clinton on a number of projects with the National Governors' Association. "He was just an extraordinarily able guy," he told me. "You couldn't work with Bill Clinton and not see it. We were philosophically in tune with each other and we took our politics seriously and it was so clear that Bill Clinton was one of the best." Dukakis knew the man giving that nominating speech was a good communicator and figured his being in front of this national audience that July night was nothing more than nervousness from a new experience.

A good nominating speech should run ten minutes. This way, you don't get tired of the speaker, and even if you do, they aren't on that much longer from the first time you start looking at your watch. Bill Clinton had been given twenty minutes and proceeded on a marathon comparable to a PBS fund drive before stopping at the thirty-two-minute mark. Shrum and I would later talk about it and he made the point that in Democratic conventions, while the cast changes over the years, they'll only listen to about five or six people: Ted Kennedy, Jesse Jackson, Mario Cuomo, the presidential nominee and the vice presidential nominee and they'll usually give the keynote a little bit of a chance. Other than that, forget about it.

But people did pay attention to the speech. House speaker and convention chairman Jim Wright had frantically signaled the Arkansas governor twice to get to the end. Clinton's close friend from law school Lanny Davis stood near the podium, running his finger under his neck. Congressman Norman Dicks of Washington later told reporters "it was the worst speech I've ever heard in my life." *Washington Post* columnist Tom Shales wrote the next day, "As Jesse Jackson electrified the hall on Tuesday, Governor Bill Clinton calcified it last night."

David Gergen, an editor at *U.S. News & World Report,* a former staffer in the Reagan White House, and a pundit for my radio show's network, the Mutual Broadcasting System, was having a late dinner in the Omni watching Bill Clinton on one of the many wide-screen televisions that were anywhere you looked (after all, Ted Turner owned the building and Ted Turner owned CNN. Some call it monopoly. I call it synergy). He would later tell me he had dinner when Clinton began and by the time Clinton finished he was having breakfast. Gergen knows everybody, which is why he is sought after to explain why something political has happened and, maybe more important, what the hell it means.

Gergen finished eating and walked over to Clinton's hotel, where he left a note in the Arkansas governor's mailbox. The note said, "Cheer up. You'll be okay and you'll come back."

I didn't spend a lot of time thinking about it other than that anyone in a Speech 101 class knows you never want to follow a kid and you always know when to shut up. That evening I was doing my national radio show and the subject never came up, which to this day I believe is significant. One of the guests was Bert Lance, who was Jimmy Carter's budget director in 1976 and, in 1988, a senior advisor to Jesse Jackson. That had been the story. Jackson let it be known he was ticked at Dukakis for announcing his selection of Texas senator Lloyd Bentsen for vice president before calling all the names on the short list for the job. And Jackson was on that list. There had been a number of meetings and phone calls between the two camps even before the convention began and I remember more than one pundit asking, "What does Jesse want?" To me it all seemed like much ado about nothing but that was the story coming out of Atlanta. Four months earlier, Jesse Jackson won the Michigan primary. He came to Atlanta with more than 1,200 delegates. So there was some basis for the attention. And the night before, Jesse spoke for fifty minutes, receiving eighteen standing ovations. Bob Shrum was right. People listen to a Jesse Jackson speech. It was one of the few moments in the Omni Arena when everyone stopped talking to hear the words. And as the speech went on, television ratings started to build.

As I was interviewing Lance, Jackson's manager, Willie Brown, was at the podium giving, in a gesture of unity, the Jackson delegates to the Dukakis camp. The fact of the matter was while Michael Dukakis had a celebrated record as the governor of Massachusetts, he needed a vice president who would complement his strengths as well as his weaknesses. Dukakis had no Washington experience. Jackson didn't have it either. But Jesse talked about a different kind of complement in that speech twenty-four hours earlier:

> The genius of America is that out of the many we become one. Providence has enabled our paths to intersect. His foreparents came to America on immigrant ships. My foreparents came to America on slave ships. But whatever the original ships, we're in the same boat tonight.

Lloyd Bentsen did have those qualities for the ticket. He had been a senator since 1971 and was chairman of the powerful Finance Committee. It was also a move to gain Reagan Democrats and the South. So when I asked Bert Lance that evening, "Can you imagine Jesse having to fulfill the role of vice president by being sent to funerals?" Bert and I laughed. Jesse Jackson wouldn't have been happy. There was more he could do from the outside, we agreed.

After the radio show that night I sat in my hotel room watching the panel discussions, the highlights of the speeches (Clinton wasn't pictured), and the floor reporters' interviews with the many high-profile delegates, all with the mute button on. After everything that had gone on that day, and there were still two days to go, I needed to spend some time with "off." But my mind was locked into anything but "off." It was racing.

I thought immediately to a scene outside the Omni that afternoon. Free enterprise exists at every political convention. There are always campaign buttons, coffee mugs with (depending on the venue) donkeys or elephants, key chains, cigarette lighters, and best of all, Jesse Jackson beach towels. You want a definition of kitsch? Go to the next convention.

Also outside the Omni was an area to protest anything that was going on inside and, as I watched, anything that *wasn't* going on inside. You know, sometimes, you just gotta get it off your chest. There was always someone wearing a sandwich board that said "Nuclear Power Is Unsafe For All Living Things" and there were a few who yelled about Ronald Reagan's policy in Nicaragua (I guess nobody told them they were in the wrong city because they were preaching to the choir here). And then there was the skinhead who stood on the risers and thanked the media for its coverage. I looked around and could only see forty or so helmeted (and grinning) riot police. This was the place where all the sandwiches short of a picnic gathered.

And there was one other thought that hit me that evening. I had been wandering throughout the convention trying to get a sense of the people and their feelings when I spied former Speaker of the House Tip O'Neill sitting in the next-to-last row. You can't miss that white mane of hair so I sat down with him for a moment or two. That's when I noticed his ID badge which gives access to the convention floor. The credential writer had spelled his name wrong (one *l* instead of two). Just eight years earlier, Tip had been chairman of the Democratic convention in New York City where Jimmy Carter sought reelection against a California governor named Ronald Reagan. Today, he was retired as speaker but still a member of the Massachusetts delegation. "Larry, life goes on," he said to me. Somehow, at that moment in the back row of this cavernous place life may indeed have been going on but it sure didn't seem fair.

Sitting in my hotel room with the world on mute, I knew there was something to be learned from all of this. Maybe it was humility and being able to acknowledge you're not running the show anymore? Maybe it was the passing of time and understanding the names do change while the issues stay the same? Maybe it was just being able to say "enough of this" on your own terms rather than on someone else's? And maybe it was all of the above?

At one of the 1,437 parties that week I ran into Senator Albert Gore Jr., who was ecstatic about the selection of Bentsen for the number two job. "A terrific pick," he said, "and the reason why I can say that is that there has been little complaining about the selection." Four years later, Bentsen said that to me about the choice of Al Gore by Bill

Clinton. Weird or prophetic or a part of the Great Plan? All of the above? I'm still not sure. And that's just fine.

I thought about a caller on the radio show that evening. He was from New York and sounded an awful lot like Joe Pesci, but then, everyone from New York sounds like Joe Pesci, so it comes down to a matter of degree and this guy had a high Pesci factor. We got into it about who George Bush was going to select as his vice president. He thought it would be Gerald Ford, which I said was one of the dumber ideas I had heard all day. And then he suggested Senator Mark Hatfield of Oregon, who I said was too far left of Bush. And then I said I really don't know who Bush will pick and, quite frankly, we're still in the middle of the Democratic convention and why would we worry about something a month away? Pesci responded saying, "Well all you guys talked about before Bentsen was who would get the nod rather than what it is Dukakis stands for and what planks are contained in his platform."

The guy was right. As soon as this convention was over late Thursday night, the first question to George Bush Friday morning would be how many names are on the list and when will the short list be made public and what are the qualifications you want in a vice president and would you consider a woman, a black, a Hispanic, a Northerner, or someone from electoral-rich California and blah blah blah ad nauseam. I knew Bush was going to be hounded and I knew when I interviewed him, if no announcement had yet been made, I'd ask the same damn question hoping he would give me the name on the air and I'd be in the headlines, maybe second paragraph below the nominee. In fact, I knew it was going to be the only thing George Bush would be asked and then the pundits and spinners would go to work saying, "Well,

Larry, the fact we don't have answers to these questions means he is indecisive, which goes along with what I've been saying all along about this guy," or conversely, "Well, Larry, this is an important matter and Mr. Bush wants to pick a vice president he knows personally because that's the way this guy operates and that goes along with what I've been saying all along, that he is a very careful man and that's what we need in these turbulent times." And who does all this? We do: the two thousand people in town to cover the other five thousand people in town.

The next morning I had a conversation with New York governor Mario Cuomo. For much of 1987, there had been a lot of talk about his possibly making a run for the White House. His name was appearing in early polling and most of the country was aware Mario could bring down the house with his speaking ability; a point everyone agreed was needed if Democrats were ever going to build a consortium of essential support from a variety of bases. Cuomo told me he had received a call from John Sasso, who was working in the Dukakis campaign, to see if he'd be willing to have an off-the-record meeting with Dukakis in Albany. Cuomo readily agreed and when the two got together one Sunday morning the Massachusetts governor told the New York governor he was thinking of running for president but would back away if Cuomo was thinking of doing the same thing.

Cuomo told Dukakis there couldn't be two Mediterranean ethnic governors from the Northeast running for the same job. And Cuomo said he was only in his first term and Dukakis was completing his second term and was smart and capable and so that was enough for him to stay out of the race. "I was getting better publicity," Cuomo told me, "but that has nothing to do with being president. I knew I could raise more money as a result of living in New York but that wasn't a good enough reason either. This wasn't any Boy Scout attitude about loyalty because I believe if I'm the best then I ought to do it. But if the other guy is as good or better, then it becomes a matter of ego. We all want people to say we are pretty but that becomes a dangerous reason to run for president. So I told Dukakis if he's serious about this, I won't give it a second thought." He was serious.

Dukakis later asked Cuomo if he wanted to give an introduction to one of the speakers at the convention. It had been a rough few weeks for the New York governor because he was in a major budget battle with the General Assembly and had delayed his travel to Atlanta in order to make sure the fiscal matters of the state were settled. As a result Cuomo declined the invitation. That morning I asked him who he would have introduced.

"Bill Clinton," he said.

"The guy who talked so long?" I asked. I knew I'd heard the name but couldn't remember the peg to which it was attached. As it turned out, I was right on the money.

"Yeah," Mario told me. "Just think, if I had been there the speeches would have gone on even longer. Maybe two hours!"

"Well he sure went on forever," I noted. "I guess that's the last we'll hear from the Arkansas governor, right?" This was the first of many times I would be wrong about Bill Clinton.

"He was agonizingly long," Cuomo said, "but don't make the mistake thinking that is a fatal error. I've known him as a governor for a long time and I think he's extremely talented. He has the strength of being able to focus. He has a single ambition, and he has always had this ambition, and it is to someday be president of the United States."

"Yeah, right," I said, the sarcasm dripping. That was the second time I was wrong about Bill Clinton.

"Larry, Clinton has a psychic karate. He can focus everything in him and can get all that power going on a single point, which is the same secret as is found in karate. For him it's being president. He's talked to people for years about it."

"I can't see it," I told him (what number we on now? 695?).

"He's a comeback kid. He ran for Congress in 1974 and got beat. He came back two years later and won the attorney general job in Arkansas. He had been burned in Arkansas [when he lost a second bid for governor in 1980] and he came back to be reelected in 1982 and served three more terms after that. He gave a lousy speech and he'll come back. He has a resilience that one can develop when singularly focused, and that has been the secret always. The things occasionally that I focus on and to which I devote my energy are the things I do best."

"Comeback kid?"

"Absolutely."

I was dubious but this wasn't an issue I was going to spend a lot of time worrying about. That night Michael Dukakis gave his acceptance speech and brought on stage all the candidates who had sought the Democratic nomination that year. Jesse Jackson was right there and grabbed hold of both Bentsen's and Dukakis's hands, which became the photo in every newspaper the next day. It was theater but the actors were sincere. It was good television with the needed clear message of unity. It was good politics but to do otherwise would have been of no benefit to anyone. It is the last act of every political convention and it is always the first activity written. It seems every campaign is designed to end this way.

One person who wasn't on the stage with Dukakis and Bentsen and Jackson and Jimmy Carter was George McGovern. He had been booked to appear on my radio show that evening and made the choice to honor his commitment. McGovern had been in Dukakis's shoes sixteen years earlier when he was the Democratic nominee to run against Richard Nixon. He had praise for the Dukakis speech while saying the Massachusetts governor offered few specifics because that's never a goal for an evening like this. Sixteen years earlier McGovern had to endure opposing views within the party and didn't get to the podium to give his acceptance speech until 3:00 A.M. Eastern Time. "The only place I made prime time," he told me, "was Guam."

It had been a rough time for the senator from South Dakota. His first choice for vice president, Missouri senator Thomas Eagleton, had been found to have undergone treatment for depression. The question spread throughout the country as to whether having a person in the number two position with a history like this was acceptable. It wasn't and McGovern had to seek another candidate. That night he told me one name his staff considered very seriously was Lloyd Bentsen. The McGovern campaign decided against him because Bentsen had just come through a bruising primary with Ralph Yarborough and the wounds from that contest may not have yet healed.

The Son of Greek Immigrants received the expected bump in the polls that Friday morning as everyone left Atlanta. Of course, the bump was based on the question, Who would you vote for if the election were today? And to my mind, this was ridiculous because George Bush hadn't even been nominated yet and the two candidates hadn't had one debate and the country had just gone through four days of nonstop Republican bashing. There were a lot of polls like this, each based on the inane idea about what the result would be if the election was held during a time other than election day. Anyone see a problem here? I didn't. I never thought about it. I was too busy talking. We all were. I recall the great American philosopher Yogi Berra commenting about a White House reception he had attended: "It was hard to have a conversation," he related, "because everyone was talking." Once again, Yogi had nailed the issue.

As has always been the case, all the talk had to stop on election day. And as is always the case, a lot of it was wrong. George Bush trounced Michael Dukakis, winning forty states. What happened? Well, I could never guess (correctly) the outcome of an Orioles game and for the same reason I could never predict (correctly) an election. Everyone is, to borrow from Jesse Jackson, in the same boat. The thing about it is this: we never learn to stop the predictions and prognostications. We will always bet the Super Bowl and the World Series and politics. I think it's in our DNA. That's why sports talk radio has a guaranteed life. It is talk based on the word "if," and "if" doesn't exist in "now," which is the whole reason it's "if" in the first place. Without that word and prognosticators to drive that word, be it political or athletic, there would be a lot of dead air. The result is, besides a lot of wrong answers, a lot of talking.

NOVEMBER 8, 1988

1988 Voting age population:	182,778,000
1988 Registration to vote:	126,379,628

LARRY KING

1988 Turnout to vote:	91,594,693
Percentage of voting age who voted:	50.11 (64-year low)
Popular vote for George Bush:	48,881,011 (426 electoral votes)
Popular vote for Michael Dukakis:	41,828,350 (111 electoral votes)

Source: Federal Election Commission

CHAPTER TWO

The
TV
Thing

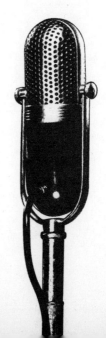

January 1992. When John F. Kennedy debated Richard Nixon for the presidency of the United States in 1960, I listened to the exchange on radio. I was driving from Tampa to Miami where I had just landed a job as a talk show host on WIOD Radio so I had listened to the entire exchange by the time I arrived at the station. Walking into the studio I mentioned to the newsman who had spent his night getting local reaction to who won that it was clear Nixon had just cleaned Kennedy's clock.

"What debate did you watch?" he asked me.

"The thing tonight with Kennedy and Nixon. Kennedy lost. I listened to this station," I said. Newsmen always want to hear that you listen to them, which, in this case, I actually had done.

"Kennedy won," he told me. "He looked better, he was energetic in his gestures, and I don't see how Nixon outdid him anywhere." Then he leaned in toward me and pointed to a television set with rabbit ears sitting on the floor in a corner of the newsroom. "This is where I took my notes on the debate. You shoulda seen it." He turned and walked into the booth for a newscast. In the days that followed I did watch portions of the debate on television and in kinescopes of what I had just heard on the radio. That was when it became clear that what one sees is sometimes different from what one hears. Kennedy *did* seem more energetic. Nixon *did* need a shave. Kennedy looked good in a dark suit against a gray background, while Nixon's gray suit blended into the background. I stood there for a moment, looked back at the gray screen in the wooden box and nodded. Radio has always been a theater of the mind but television was a theater, period. You came into the room, sat down and watched. In theory, the picture tells you what to see. No, I didn't think of all this as I stood in the Miami studio that evening. It took a while, like until now. But to show how we've progressed, today we watch the same show and then argue about what we've seen. I guess just because the picture tells you what to see doesn't mean that's what you, or anyone else, will see.

Three years later all of America was watching the television set. And John F. Kennedy was once again the reason but, this time, it was because he had been assassinated. I still see those days as black-and-white. It's because that's how we saw it on television. This was the beginning of television being a center around which we gathered to learn and to mourn and to be afraid and to be reassured. My set stayed on for all of those four days. A lot of televisions did.

Kennedy's son, John Jr., told me he had no recollection at all of the funeral (he was three at the time). In fact, he knew his father only through television. And thirty-plus years later we again gathered; this time on a July Saturday morning to learn John Jr. was missing. Across the country, indeed across the world, people reflected on their visions of the president's son. Most of those images came from television and now, in this tragedy of an airplane crash off Martha's Vineyard in which John, his wife, Carolyn, and her sister, Lauren, died, television replayed John Jr.'s salute, the scene under his father's desk in the Oval Office, and the launching of his magazine, *George*. For most of us, that's how we knew him. I was fortunate that our paths had crossed a number of times; the last being when he had appeared as a guest on *Larry King Live*. After the interview he and his wife decided they would go back to New York rather than stay in Washington for the night. CNN was two blocks away from Union Station and I remember John strapping a backpack over his suit, taking his wife's hand, and saying they'd walk to the train. No car, no escort, no entourage. He shook my hand saying, "Thank you, Mr. King." He always called me Mr. King.

I had told him about the first time I met his father. It was 1958 and I was driving one Sunday morning with three other guys from a Miami radio station where we all worked. We were cruising along and looking at mansions when out of nowhere—BAM! I hit a car in front of me. I get out and the driver of the car I hit gets out and we look at the minimal, thank God, damage. I offer to give my name and driver's license number and all that and the guy holds up his hand and says, "Forget it." He looks at the dented rear bumper on his car and then looks at me.

"How can you do this?" he begins. "How can you hit me when it's a Sunday morning and we're the only cars on the road and, more than that, we're going in the same direction? How is that possible?"

25

I had no answer and that's what I told him. Then he reaches out to shake my hand as well as the hands of everyone in my car who, by that time, were also standing on the street surveying the damage. "I'm John Kennedy," he says, "and in two years I'm going to run for president and all I ask is that you guys vote for me." John Jr. laughed at the story and said he had heard similar tales about his father's longstanding political ambition. We both agreed it reminded us of a fellow from Arkansas.

We gathered all that July weekend and for part of the following week as divers searched for the wreckage. During that time we debated whether John Jr. should have been flying, whether the Navy should be involved in the search operations, and if there was a Kennedy curse, and the conspirators had a chance to offer their idea that the plane was taken down as part of Castro's revenge against his father's attempts to knock him off. We gather whenever a news story breaks and this is the reason we provide seemingly nonstop coverage. Every time I give a speech, the same question is asked: Why do you guys have to overdo everything? My answer is a simple one: Just tell me how much is enough. Tell me when that point occurs. The response is "I don't know," which is, I guess, the right answer. That's where we are. The difference between the days of Walter Cronkite and the three network channels and today is that we have five hundred different places to get our information and, should we choose, five hundred different places not to get information. That's progress. I think.

Gathering has changed. George Bush's press secretary, Marlin Fitzwater, told me there were many times the president would watch Saddam Hussein on television during the war with Iraq. And Bush knew Saddam did the same when he was talking to reporters in the White House Briefing Room. Today, gathering has expanded to include not just constituents, but opponents as well.

On January 26, 1992, Americans once again were gathered for what has become an annual event. CBS had the Super Bowl, which featured the Washington Redskins and the Buffalo Bills. I had been invited to accompany the owner of the Redskins, Jack Kent Cooke (who always got the table I used at Duke Zeibert's when he was in town), and, of course, Duke (who always gave the table to Cooke if he was in town). The Skins won 37–24, holding the Bills' running back Thurman Thomas to only thirteen yards. I came away from that game with two thoughts: Cooke's table had just become Cooke's Table and even if he was on business in Romania, it would be left empty because he owned it. The other idea I had was that Redskins quarterback Mark Rypien would make a great interview for the show the next night when I was back in Washington, since he had just been named Most Valuable Player.

I had been to the celebration party with Duke and Jack Kent Cooke and, as a result, wasn't one of the millions who gathered that Sunday to watch *60 Minutes*, which came on right after the Super Bowl. I knew Bill Clinton was going to answer questions about a woman and I knew it was coming at a strategic moment in his campaign to be president. That was it. When I got back to my hotel that evening, I followed what has become a routine whenever walking into a room: turn on the lights and pick up the clicker and turn on the TV (I'm able to do this in any city and with any television: Sony, Philips, Magnavox, Panasonic—doesn't matter). I caught the late news and, of course, the lead story was the

Redskins win. And then we came to the second story: There was Bill Clinton and Hillary Clinton and Steve Kroft and any thought of my interviewing Rypien went out the door. I knew right away this was going to be *the* story for a while. I knew something else: This was the end of Bill Clinton.

Less than twenty-four hours later I was in the Washington studio. And the country, once again, gathered to learn. The focus of the show wasn't just that Clinton might have had an affair, but the way we learned about it: The *Star*, a tabloid, had first carried the story about Gennifer Flowers and her alleged twelve-year affair with Clinton. And they paid her for it. Then, for those who declared they never read a tabloid, the legitimate press such as *60 Minutes* and *Nightline* used it. So we were talking about how trash knows no boundaries and about why everyone was now up and running with a tabloid story. The panel included David Osborne, who had advised the Clinton campaign on domestic issues. He was furious at the events of the past day:

> This is a new low for American journalism. We have
> a story in the tabloids and the rules of journalistic
> ethics are when an unreliable publication prints
> something you don't repeat it, you don't mention it,
> until you've independently verified that. The *New
> York Post* immediately violated it.

The frenzy was back. The story had sex, power, and the possible destruction of a promising future. And we had what seemed to be an attempt to say it wasn't so. When the hour was over the arguments kept going among the guests. This had been one of those shows that just took off with a life of its own. That's what happens in a frenzy. There were a lot of shows like this in 1992. And 1994. And certainly 1998.

Two weeks later, on the night of the New Hampshire primary, George Bush won with 53 percent of the vote. The story, however, was Pat Buchanan coming in second with 37 percent. Just a year earlier, Bush had high approval ratings for Desert Storm even though Saddam Hussein still had a job and an army. On the other side of the aisle, Paul Tsongas beat Bill Clinton 33 percent to 25 percent. That night, Clinton addressed his supporters saying "I want you to know in November we are going to win a great victory against Pat Buchanan." One thing you could say about the Arkansas governor: He wasn't giving up. Buchanan had momentum. And the following night, we talked about where it could take him.

> KING: You know, Ross Perot is our guest
> tomorrow night. Would he be someone
> you'd consider for vice president?
> BUCHANAN: I'll tell you, someone sent a
> speech by Ross Perot and it was pure
> dynamite. Let me tell you, one of my
> themes is it's not simply the Democrats
> anymore. It's not simply the Republicans.
> There's a one-party government here in
> Washington and I think the establishment
> of both parties needs to be shaken up,
> turned over, and you need some fresh new
> people.

My first impression was "yeah, right, Pat." But then, it seemed he might be on to something. Maybe we needed

29

someone who would turn the entire election process on its side or at least let us get under the hood to take a look at why it isn't running very well? "Going under the hood" wasn't a phrase I had ever used to describe political reform. That soon changed.

The next morning my phone rang and I remember hearing the Nashville accent before understanding any of the words that were going to follow. The voice belonged to a guy I had heard about but never before met: Thomas J. Hooker. He had run for governor of Tennessee and lost. He had run for senator from Tennessee and lost. He was as successful as a businessman as he was unsuccessful as a politician. And he told me to ask Ross Perot about running for president.

"Ross is on to talk about the economy," I told him.

"Ask him. I think he'll do it," Hooker pleaded. I knew Perot had been thinking about it. Earlier, he told a Tennessee radio station it was a possibility. And my producer, Tammy Haddad, had been encouraging him to appear. More than a year earlier, Perot had been on to argue against military action in Kuwait. It was clear he connected with viewers; not just with his straight talk but also in his approach that people deserve better than what they've got. So, twelve hours after my phone call with Hooker, that's how I opened the show:

> KING: Are you going to run?
> PEROT: No.
> KING: Flat "no"?
> PEROT: But we've got an hour to talk about
> the real problems that face this nation and
> you, in effect, have sort of an electronic

town hall, so I think we can serve the
country by really getting down in the
trenches, talking about what we have to do
and then doing it.

Okay, I thought to myself, Hooker is unsuccessful in the
prediction business too. I pressed some more but the same
question was getting the same answer.

Perot told me he was a fixer. He said the people own the
country and the only way to assess blame was to look in the
mirror. He began his arguments with the popular "Now here's
the thing, Larry . . ." and "Step one . . ." And he took us under
the hood to say that while the candidates agree we need some
"jump-starting," what the country really needs is a funda-
mental fix. He wanted an electronic town hall and said *Larry
King Live* was pretty close to the way one would operate. It
was ringing through the air. I could feel it. And during a
quiet moment in a commercial break, I thought back twenty-
four hours and the words Pat Buchanan used about needing
new ideas and "fresh new people." The floor director counted
me out of the break and as he did it, I thought to myself,
"We're almost out of time. What the hell. Try again." So before we went on the air, I leaned over and said, "Ross, I'm
gonna ask one more time. This is it. Otherwise, what are you
doing here?" We came out of the break and I looked him in
the eye. It was the best question I ever asked, even though
it took fifty minutes to get an answer:

> KING: By the way, is there *any* scenario in
> which you'd run for president? Can you give
> me a scenario in which you say, "Okay, I'm
> in"?

PEROT: Number one: I don't want to.

KING: I know, but is there a scenario—

PEROT: Number two, you know nobody's been luckier than I have. And number three, I've got all these everyday folks that make the world go round writing me in longhand—

KING: Is there a scenario?

PEROT: Now that touches me. But I don't want to fail them. That would be the only thing that would interest me and so I would simply say to them and all these folks who are constantly calling and writing, if you feel so strongly about this, number one—

I thought to myself, "Stop with the numbers already and say it." Ross was looking directly at the camera now. We had less than three minutes remaining.

PEROT: —I will not run as a Democrat or a Republican because I will not sell out to anybody but the American people—and I will sell out to them.

KING: So you'd run as an independent?

PEROT: Number two, if you're that serious, you the people are that serious, you register me in fifty states and if you are not willing to organize and do the—

KING: Wait a minute! Are you saying— Wait a minute!

He was in. But Ross kept adding conditions and I wondered if this is what he's like when negotiating a deal: You spend eight weeks getting to yes and by the time you arrive you are glad but even gladder that it's over. As soon as the show ended, we shook hands and he leaned toward me. "You don't think anything is going to happen, do you?" he asked.

"Ross," I said, "you just never know."

At that moment, a bellman at the hotel where Ross was staying had just finished watching the interview. He went to Perot's room and slipped an envelope with $5 in it under the door. Ross Perot had just received his first campaign contribution. Maybe Pat Buchanan's words about the need to shake up the process with a new face and ideas had finally landed. The face, however, was different than anyone, including Pat, expected.

In fact, it took a while for me to understand what had happened in that hour. Weeks later in airports complete strangers would come up to me and ask, "Hey Larry, can you tell Ross I'm gonna vote for the first time in eight years?" And I remember going to George Will's annual party, which always occurs just before opening day of the baseball season. The Ross story had been out there for more than a month by that time and both Will and Sam Donaldson teased me that afternoon. "You brought him in," they said, and I remember throwing it back at them with a simple defense: All I did was ask him questions. If he was viable, then he did that without me.

The man I predicted was politically dead in January proceeded to win key Super Tuesday victories in Florida, Louisiana, Mississippi, Tennessee, and Texas. I still hadn't gotten a chance to interview Bill Clinton despite daily conversations my staff was having with his campaign (as well as that of George Bush). The White House line was it isn't "presidential" for Bush to take phone calls. I wasn't buying this at all. The same reasoning came from the White House in requests for the president to appear on my radio show. It was frustrating because I could see the lack of logic. Years later, I talked off the air to Bush's press secretary, Marlin Fitzwater, about it:

> It was a tough call. Before this time the guiding
> principle had been if you are an incumbent president
> you have the advantage of stature. . . . Frankly we
> were slow to pick up on it. Clinton didn't care.
> Clinton didn't have anything to lose. What we
> discovered was Clinton was making it work for him,
> so that we had to take the chance.

Marlin was right. On the week that Clinton nailed the last-needed delegate to guarantee a trip to New York for the Democratic nomination, he spent an hour with Dan Rather answering questions from viewers. The next day he showed up on Arsenio Hall's late-night TV show in shades with a saxophone. Arsenio had an audience that everyone else had been talking about for months as "disaffected" or "disenfranchised" or just "dissed" about politics. The fact of the matter was nobody had ever tried to reach them other than through dry public service announcements about the importance of getting involved in the political process. The dissed were expected to go to the party rather than the party go to the dissed. When you think about it, this was a lousy way to increase participation. Clinton took questions about the Elvis Stamp, voter apathy, and racism. It was clear he connected and it was just the beginning. Interestingly enough, President

Bush held a hastily called news conference the next day. The White House was catching on.

That very evening, I had my first opportunity to talk with Clinton. I was in the Washington studio and he was at the Governor's Mansion in Little Rock. As we waited to go on the air I did a quick voice check to make sure he could hear me and that I could hear him.

"How you doing, Mr. Governor?" I asked.

Clinton looked right at the camera. "Larry King. Well, well, well." He smiled. "I used to listen to you late at night here in Arkansas. And now here I am."

I didn't say it but my thoughts went immediately to what seemed an obvious question after half a year of hearing about women. "And what, Mr. Clinton, were you doing while you listened to me on the radio?" That was the moment I took the cue from the floor director and we were off and running. Clinton covered health care, the deficit, foreign policy, and even his TV appearance twenty-four hours earlier.

> CALLER: I was just curious about the motives
> behind Mr. Clinton appearing on the
> Arsenio Hall show and if he wonders if that
> might have the same effect on him or his
> campaign as it did to Michael Dukakis
> getting into the tank?
> KING: The playing the clarinet I guess is the
> question. Do you think that was kind of
> light stuff?

I should add right here the majority of the mail I received as a result of that show wasn't about the interview with the man who was going to become the Democratic candidate for president of the United States. It was about why I was such an idiot that I can't tell the difference between a saxophone and a clarinet. The answer is, it beats me.

> CLINTON: Well, it *was* light stuff. I respect Arsenio Hall. He invited me to come on his show. He has a young audience of nonvoters, a lot of people who don't vote, whose lives are at stake in this election, who are worried about their country and their future.

We were now a little more than a month away from the Democratic convention, so I asked the always necessary question about whether or not he had picked a vice president. It did seem to me that the Veep Question was being asked even sooner than ever—if that was possible. Things sure were moving faster these days. And it allowed the talking heads, which I admit to watching all the time, opportunities to prognosticate about potential vice presidential candidates on the basis of geography or potential electoral votes. Clinton said he had shortened the list but wouldn't bite on any of the possibilities I threw at him, which included Bill Bradley, who had taken himself out of any running for president. Clinton said he wasn't going to be put under any time constraints. When you think about it, it's an insane question. Never has there been a candidate who has said to me, "Well yes, Larry, as a matter of fact I have made the decision," and proceeded to name names. I don't think that will ever change. And yeah, I'm going to keep asking.

Less than two weeks later I was talking to Bill Clinton again. He had met with visiting Russian president Boris

Yeltsin at Blair House just across the street from the White House. I thought it interesting that a visiting head of state would take the time to meet with a possible head of state but, like I say, these were different times. Maybe Boris Yeltsin was aware George Bush was having trouble in the polls, which came out every two seconds, so he decided to cover all the bases. But this interview taught me something about Bill Clinton.

> KING: What did Boris Yeltsin have to say today?
>
> CLINTON: He said he had been up and down in politics. He'd never quit. And he said whatever happens in this election or the next one or the next one, it's important just to stick by your convictions. That's what I like about him. He's not a quitter. His political obituary has been written many times but he genuinely believed in something bigger than himself.

Hanging in there was a quality by which the country had come to know Bill Clinton. He stayed on course despite "bimbo eruptions," as they came to be called. My impression after the second interview was this guy had staying power. And that's an admirable quality for anyone sitting in the Oval Office.

In case you are wondering, yeah, I asked the Veep Question again. No decision. I figured it this way: Since he was from Arkansas, the veep was going to come from the North to provide a needed geographic balance to the ticket. Just before the Democratic convention, Clinton announced that

37

Senator Al Gore from neighboring Tennessee was the choice. Being wrong about Bill Clinton was becoming a second career for me.

Prior to that year's Republican convention, Dan Quayle spent an hour talking with me about his four years as the vice president and why voters should give him another four to complete the Bush-Quayle agenda. I always liked Quayle but I thought our introduction to him four years earlier in New Orleans when the Indiana senator bounded up on the stage as George Bush announced him to be the Running Mate was not exactly what we would envision for the guy holding the second-in-command position. And Quayle got knocked unmercifully. And unfairly. In a number of interviews I had with him since, it has always been clear the guy knows his stuff. So I was looking forward to sitting down with him one more time.

The Supreme Court had upheld a Pennsylvania law requiring parental consent before a minor could have an abortion. Quayle had praised the decision, saying it was a move in the right direction. And since we were less than a month before the Republican convention, which had a plank in its platform advocating a constitutional amendment banning abortion, I asked Quayle about it.

KING: What if your daughter came to you with
      that problem all fathers fear?
QUAYLE: I hope I never have to deal with it.
      But obviously I would counsel her and talk
      to her and support her on whatever decision
      she made.
KING: And if the decision were abortion?

QUAYLE: I'd support my daughter. I'd hope she
wouldn't make that decision.

All hell broke loose after that interview. And I walked
off the set saying to the staff we made news. "Did you hear
it?" I asked Tammy Haddad, my producer. "He said if Perot
supporters vote for Clinton then they should split their tick-
ets and vote for a Republican Congress. We're gonna be the
lead story again."

"Larry," she said, "that wasn't the news."

Tammy was right. Suddenly, Quayle's answers were thrown
to his wife, who was interviewed on a Des Moines radio station. She said if Corinne became pregnant, she would take
the child to term. The vice president was in Indiana the next
day and said there had been no change in his position on
abortion. Bill Clinton was asked what he'd do if Chelsea became pregnant and said he wouldn't talk to the press about
it, which was probably the best answer of the entire escapade.
There was no mention of ticket splitting. I thought Quayle
had answered honestly about offering support and I gotta say
I still don't see how ticket splitting wasn't the story out of
that interview.

While the Clinton campaign was on a roll, Ross Perot
was having trouble. Big trouble. He had gone to Nashville
for a speech before the NAACP, parts of which the audience
took to be insulting. I'm positive he didn't mean it that way
but the damage was done. Poll numbers were dropping. By
the end of the Democratic convention in New York City,
which was as boring as the Republican convention because,
again, we knew the result, Ross made a decision he would
later tell me was a mistake. He got out. It was complete

surprise. If 1992 had been a TV script, it couldn't have been written without an editor saying "this just isn't believable."

The next morning the *New York Post* had a photo of Ross with the headline "What A Wimp." That night he was back in the studio with me.

> KING: Why?
>
> PEROT: I looked carefully at the facts. The greatest concern I have is to deliver the goods for the people. Once we are in a three-way race, it would wind up in the House of Representatives. There are not so many independents in the House so—
>
> KING: But you knew that going in, Ross—
>
> PEROT: I know but I didn't think it would be a three-way race. My whole plan was that we could win in November.

I could tell Ross had been through a lot. And I asked him about the 148 days since February 20 when so many things changed in just an hour. Ross said he wasn't aware how "vicious and petty it was inside the tent."

> KING: It looks like, or is perceived by many, that when you leave it you're saying, "Hey that's the way the tent is. I told you I could fight the tent. I can't fight the tent."
>
> PEROT: I have said that I don't believe the proper course of action is to have me run as president. I do believe the proper course of action is take all of these talented creative people that have mobilized themselves

across the country and use that to correct
the problems inside the tent.

While a lot of people later told me they watched this interview and didn't believe Ross was worried about the election being thrown into the House and the real reason was
he just didn't want to go through the crap anymore, I kept
an open mind while sitting with him. I was in shock at what
had happened over the past twenty-four hours but, at the
same time, I was willing to just listen and watch and, maybe,
learn from what had just happened. Even today I look back
at the ninety minutes with Ross that summer night and accept his words at face value. But I know that headline in the
New York Post hurt him.

When the show ended, I could tell Ross was feeling a lot
better than when we began. Still, at lunch the next day, people came up to me saying, "What's wrong with that guy?" I
didn't know the answer. I didn't even know if there *was* anything wrong. Ross is complicated. So are a lot of successful
people.

The thing about this business is how fast things happen.
Perot was in and then he was at the top and then he was
gone. George Bush had been unbeatable a year earlier and
now was fighting for his political life. Bill Clinton had begun
the year as damaged goods and now he had the nomination.
And in each case I had been flat-out wrong. In each case I
looked at the "now" and said to myself, "That's it" or "Nothing is going to change" or "Tomorrow doesn't matter." Here
is what I learned in 1992: It ain't tomorrow as much as it's
the next moment. That's what I mean about things speeding
up. News travels faster. That's the easy part. Predicting it,
forget about it. Reacting to it, that's what takes some time.

There was a lot of reacting to do. Perot was back in one month before the November election. When I heard it, I just shook my head. I didn't think 1992 could get any weirder. And when I heard the news about Ross, I stopped thinking about the year and that adjective in the same sentence.

But since we are on the subject of weird, "the talk show campaign" was in full swing. Newspaper columnists had been using that phrase since Clinton's Arsenio Hall appearance a few months earlier. And I was getting requests from all over the country to lecture at journalism schools and before private organizations to explain the phenomenon and answer questions about why I decided to put political candidates on my television show. The demands of both television and radio kept me from accepting any of these offers, which was a good thing. You see, I'd have accepted the invitations, taken the speaking fee, appeared as scheduled, and said, "Folks, I have no idea what's happening because I'm not doing anything different than I've done for the past thirty years." There would have been a lot of time for questions and answers.

With five weeks to go before election day, George Bush and Bill Clinton and Ross Perot were all doing interviews and, in most cases, taking phone calls. Bush agreed to a taped interview on a Sunday at the White House. This meant no phone calls. I thought that was a mistake but was grateful to have the chance to ask some questions of the president. And I figured it this way: It's a beginning.

> BUSH: I hope you understand that we've just
> resisted call-ins in the White House. Maybe
> I'm overly respectful of the trust that
> Barbara and I have to keep this place as
> dignified as possible. But I look forward to

coming on your show and answering any
questions they can throw—curveballs,
straight balls, fastballs.

I didn't agree but I wasn't going to pursue it with the
president of the United States right outside the Lincoln Bed-
room. He was an interesting guy and I was eager to ask some
questions. Bush had talking points for the interview, one of
which was the bad rap he was getting every single day. It was
media-bashing time and it's something that is always the topic
when things aren't going well inside the Beltway. You go after
the messenger instead of looking at the message. Bush was
double digits behind Bill Clinton.

BUSH: One thing about the campaign, these
final stages, the debates: You can take your
case to the American people. I have not
been happy with the press, but that's not—
I'm not going to dwell on that.

KING: But you also—isn't it true that you—
Did you miss the recession, or did it come
late? Are you insulated here, and didn't see
it? What happened in that?

BUSH: Well, that's a charge that maybe I was
being too technical. The national definition
of a recession, I believe, is two consecutive
quarters of negative growth.

KING: Yes.

BUSH: Your listeners may have trouble
believing this: We have had five quarters of
positive growth in a row. So, when I said,
"There isn't a recession" last fall,

technically, I was right. But I should have done it recognizing that there's a hell of a lot of people hurting.

Twenty-four hours later I was in Ocala, Florida, with Governor Clinton and Al Gore, who were on a bus trip to gather votes. It was a crisp evening and there was a crowd of more than two hundred people gathered around us. I kept thinking how different this was from my location just a day earlier. And while I have always been impressed walking through the White House and wishing a painting or a chair could tell just one story when you realize the history that has occurred inside those walls, I was, in all honesty, more interested in being outside with the people yelling and the temperature dropping and the wind speed increasing. This ain't exactly a common feeling for a Jew from Brooklyn but I could feel the energy in the air, literally.

Part of the energy was coming from James Carville, the Clinton campaign's fast-talking strategist, who was always available to spin a story. He was dressed in jeans everywhere he went. Later, I remember him coming to both my radio and television show dressed the same way after spending hours in high-level meetings with the president. On that day, with the campaign still in full swing, James waved and we spent a few minutes talking baseball before the interview. And I told him about all the offers I was getting to speak about talk shows and the fact I had nothing to say because nothing, as far as I could tell, had changed. Carville cut in as he is wont to do when he disagrees.

"Larry, you may be doing the same thing but the world outside your studio is changing. Hell, Willie Sutton was asked why he robbed banks and he said that's where the money could be found. The governor and Perot and, finally, the president, are all going on talk shows because that's where the voters can be found."

The ninety minutes with Clinton and Gore in Ocala went fast. We covered issues ranging from the House and Senate overriding President Bush's veto of the cable bill, the economy, the efforts to find out what happened to MIAs from Vietnam and, of course, the effect of Ross Perot on the election. And we talked about something called NAFTA—the North American Free Trade Agreement— among the U.S., Canada, and Mexico—which Clinton said needed more work before he could be on board. When the show was over, Clinton and Gore went into the crowd and shook every hand, holding conversations and asking questions.

Two days later I was sitting with President Bush again, this time in San Antonio, where he had, that very afternoon, signed the NAFTA proposal with President Salinas of Mexico. All it needed now was ratification in Congress. The White House was pleased with the interview he had done with me Sunday night so the decision was made to get him out of the Oval Office. A series of debates were about to take place among the three candidates and this was a good time for him to interact with real people. Bush told me, though, he wasn't particularly excited about doing a debate.

> KING: How much do you think, Mr. President,
>   is dependent on these debates?
> BUSH: I don't know. I think some, but not
>   all. I don't know that a debate has ever
>   decided anything. They always cite the

45

Kennedy-Nixon debates, where people listening to it on radio thought Nixon won, and people watching it thought Kennedy won. But I don't know. We don't think that it's, you know, the be-all and end-all, but it does give you the chance to stand up there and say "Here's what I'm for." No filters. People don't need a Monday morning quarterback [saying] "you have just heard this or that."

Bush did well. And I could tell he enjoyed the back and forth with callers while talking to the audience and shaking hand after hand. In fact, one caller from Cleveland asked Bush where he was a resident. The president said Texas.

KING: And still a Texas driver's license?

BUSH: Still. You want to see it?

KING: Yes. Make sure it isn't expired.

BUSH: No, no, it's not expired. (He pulls out his wallet and hands it over to me.)

KING: I like the smile!

BUSH: Does it say "President"?

KING: Wait a minute. Yep. President George W. Bush. The White House, 1600 Pennsylvania Avenue, Department of Public Safety, Texas. It's a class C driver's license.

BUSH: Hey, wait a minute.

KING: Six feet, one inch tall. Sex is male. Eyes are brown. Birth date is 6/12/24. And this expires 6/1/93.

BUSH: I'm legal. Where's your car. Let's go for
a drive.

It was the first time I had seen George Bush loosen up.
And I left San Antonio the next morning thinking not about
the interview as much as about these three men who want
to be president of the United States. They spend millions of
dollars and thousands of hours to get there. And when one
of them does, that person loses the chance to walk down a
street and talk to someone whose name they don't know
about what is and isn't working. And it is those conversations that make each of these men, and the forty-one men
before them who have achieved this goal, want the job in
the first place. Each has an idea of how to make something
work better. How, I wondered, might the country be different if bus trips and forums and shaking hands could be a part
of every day for every person who sits in the Oval Office? I
knew I'd never know the answer.

Those who are paid to watch television and complain
were busy as the Talk Show Campaign started winding down.
Jonathan Yardley, book critic of the *Washington Post*, and a
fellow I have always enjoyed reading, took all of society to
task for allowing a presidential campaign to fall to the level
of talk show hosts interviewing candidates. "To put it bluntly,"
he wrote on October 12, "these aren't the people who ought
to be asking the questions." I kept reading that line over and
over and getting madder and madder. I was in my condo in
Arlington, Virginia, thinking, "Well, Mr. Yardley, does that
mean Rather and Jennings and Brokaw are the only ones
who *should* be asking the questions? And if it's wrong for a
television talk show host to ask the questions, why *isn't* it

wrong for a book critic at the *Washington Post* to be writing a column about what television should and shouldn't do?" For the first time, the idea became real that a media elite existed. And I knew I was getting hammered and Donahue was getting hammered and Arsenio was getting hammered because the smug journalists inside the Beltway were watching their readers and viewers looking at other areas for information. They didn't like it. And like in some political campaigns, they went after the messenger. It was a recurring theme in 1992.

Despite Mr. Yardley's handwringing, Bush and Clinton and Perot were everywhere now, spending an hour on the morning shows, taking phone calls (and good questions), and doing it all without the "filter" George Bush talked about earlier. And by the last week of the campaign, Bush had narrowed the double-digit gap according to polls. Now the country was focused on something called the "Perot Factor." It was pretty clear Ross wasn't going to win this thing, but nobody had ever seen a third party candidate with $60 million to spend on infomercials with charts and graphs. In some markets, Perot was beating network television shows. The undecided vote, however, was the number everyone was trying to gauge. The Perot Factor was playing havoc with any firm ideas any pollster or pundit or, for that matter, talk show host might have.

Dan Quayle came on in that final run and, to my enjoyment, brought a chart of his own. It showed the economy was completing six straight quarters of growth. And when I asked why people weren't feeling good about the numbers on his graph, we got into the coverage and how 98 percent of all stories about the economy during the past month were negative. I could feel my eyes start to roll back into my head.

KING: Have you ever seen two newspapermen
    say, "Let's go get Bush today"? I've never
    seen that. Never.
QUAYLE: (laughs) You know—
KING: Where they plot to hurt someone?
    Where, like, some nefarious conspiracy—
QUAYLE: No, I'm not getting into a nefarious
    conspiracy, but what I am saying is that
    they're saying "Okay, let's see. Do we want
    to do a positive story or a negative story on
    the economy?" And, obviously, there has
    been a calculated decision made with those
    that control what goes on television, control
    what goes on the networks, to make it a
    negative story.

I knew of no editorial board or broadcast editor that have
had conversations about steering stories one way because the
other party has been in office for twelve years, a point Quayle
made in the interview. It reminded me of a caller to the radio
show who said late one evening, "You know, Larry, every time
the space shuttle goes up, it rains six weeks later." The logic
was the same. There wasn't any.

Ross Perot had adopted the Patsy Cline song "Crazy" at
every campaign stop. He had been the topic of a 60 *Minutes*
piece looking into his claim there was a concentrated effort
by the Republican party to disrupt his daughter's wedding.
And when we had our last sit down in Washington I asked
him about it.

PEROT: Larry, just—Look, let's just go back to
    the issues that concern the people. The

49

only reason I have done this, the only
reason I have put my family through this—

KING: But you've become a public—You're a
major public figure, Ross.

PEROT: I know. I am their servant. I am here
to serve them. I am here for one reason,
and that is to fix the problems that face
this nation. It's the only reason I'm doing it.
My family is totally supportive. The minute
my daughter got back from her wedding, we
told her. We didn't tell her until after the
wedding trip. And her reaction was—she's a
very strong person—she says, "Okay, the
wedding's over. Let's get back in the race."

When the show was over, Ross wouldn't make any predictions about whether he was going to work next Wednesday at Perot Systems in Dallas or, as he had promised if
elected, in Washington, D.C. We shook hands, slapped each
other on the back, and walked off the set. That's when we
were met by two uniformed police officers saying there had
been a bomb threat phoned in and the building was being
evacuated immediately. The news operation at that hour
comes out of Atlanta so the Washington bureau isn't affected
too much. Still, it was a weird feeling to think someone had
felt so strongly about something they wanted to kill Ross—
or was it me? All of this is going through my head as I walk
out the door and down the stairs and out the lobby and to
my car. No, I didn't stick around to say goodbye. Not to Ross,
not to the desk clerks. Nobody. I learned that Ross told the
D.C. cops to get out of the building and not risk harming
themselves, which could, in turn, harm their families.

During that week the radio program moved to daytime for a special series of political shows before the election. We took calls from Clinton and Perot's campaign manager and Bush's campaign officials. And we took a call from Texas where a fourth-grade class was listening as part of its current events lesson. Senator Tim Wirth (D-Col) was in the studio having decided not to seek reelection. We polled the class: Clinton 45 percent, Bush 30 percent, and Perot 25 percent. I remember laughing at the numbers as I wrote them down.

It had been a long campaign. Clinton lost his voice, Ross was going nonstop, and Bush had a horrible cold. Even in this electronic age, there remains a need to do what worked in Iowa; to look at the voters, to shake their hands and say (if the candidate can still talk), "I need your help." Everyone bitched about the last few days, including me, but I also knew it was better this way than sitting in a sterile television studio talking to one city and then another and then another. In that last week, the TV show decided to go all out and talk to each candidate one more time, showing the voters just who these three guys were and what each wanted to do if given the job. They were all more than happy to find an hour or so to talk to a national audience, despite trying to be in ten different places every twenty-four hours.

The president and I had a final interview in front of an audience at Memorial Hall in Racine, Wisconsin, on the Friday before the election. As we went on the air, Ronald Reagan's secretary of defense, Caspar Weinberger, had been reindicted by a Grand Jury impaneled by Special Prosecutor Lawrence Walsh (Weinberger and five others in the Iran-contra case were pardoned by President Bush on Christmas Eve, 1992). The timing couldn't have been worse for Bush and his campaign let the point be known. While I understood their suspicions, I also wondered where the solution was to be found. Does the special prosecutor go on vacation during a campaign? If so, the guy only works one day a year. Still, the Justice Department isn't supposed to do anything that can affect an election so I understood Bush's concern, even though it was his Justice Department. The issue centered on questions regarding whether Weinberger knew about an Israeli-brokered agreement to buy four thousand TOW missiles that went to moderate elements in Iran in exchange for five U.S. hostages in Lebanon. The question was whether George Bush knew about the scheme. He said no. Clinton charged there was "a smoking gun" in the role Bush played as vice president.

Clinton's campaign manager, George Stephanopoulos, called our Washington studio as the interview progressed and was transferred to Tammy Haddad, who was on site in the production truck outside Memorial Hall. She listened to George complain about me not asking tough questions. This was part of the work done in the now famous "war room" where television, radio, and magazines and newspapers were called by Clinton campaign staff and told, among other things, to ask tougher questions of whatever Bush official was being interviewed. Tammy told Stephanopoulos she was in the middle of a live show, Larry has asked all the right questions, and she couldn't listen to any more of his complaints. However, she added, if he wanted to ask Bush a question, do it now. Stephanopoulos put her on hold for a second and then came back on, saying okay.

STEPHANOPOULOS: It says quite clearly in the memo five hostages in return for the sale of four thousand TOWs to Iran by

Israel. How could you not know that it was arms-for-hostages?

BUSH: May I refer you to the wonderful sleuthing done by the United States Congress, costing the taxpayers millions of dollars, where the accurate records are reflected here? And if that was Caspar Weinberger's opinion, fine. Go ask President Reagan if he thought it was arms-for-hostages—same transaction—and he'd say "No."

KING: But if four thousand TOWs are going in return for five hostages, what else could it be?

BUSH: Larry, please read the testimony. There's all— There was kind of trying to work with moderates. They weren't dealing with the people who had the hostages. There's a whole history that this poor guy is trying to resurrect four days before the election. It's wonderful how his call gets in, this random call—a woman from Belgium, one from Switzerland— It's perfectly all right.

Members of the Bush campaign complain to this day it was a setup. It wasn't. They say the election was lost as a result of that interview. It wasn't and they know it.

At 10:48 P.M. election night it was official. Bill Clinton had gathered 43 percent of the vote, George Bush 37 percent, and Ross Perot 19 percent. But the number impressing me the most was the turnout. More than 55 percent of Americans went to the polls. And the fourth graders in Houston were more accurate than any pundit I had interviewed for the entire year.

The next day I was reading the newspapers in my living room and looking forward to interviews with people who aren't running for office. Of course we'd do a lot of pundit-driven shows for the next few days trying to put into words what had happened, but it was a good feeling to know I would soon be talking to Don Rickles instead of some political something or another. That was my thought as the phone rang. I knew the voice right away.

"Larry?"

"How about you come on and talk about the year, Ross?" I offered.

"Larry, that's not why I'm calling."

"Okay, what's up?"

"Larry, there's a lady in the hospital who likes your show. And she's real sick. I think a phone call from you would make her feel good." He gave me the phone number and one minute later I'm talking to a very surprised lady named Helen. That moment taught me more about Ross Perot than anything else the entire year.

When I think about 1992 there are any number of scenes that come to mind. I remember the speed of change, the anger in the voters, the fact you just can't dismiss anything anymore because anything does, indeed, go. And I have one other thought: Ross wasn't kidding when he said the day after the 1992 election he would be at work.

NOVEMBER 3, 1992

1992 Voting age population:	89,529,000
1992 Registration to vote:	133,821,178
1992 Turnout to vote:	104,405,155

Percentage of voting age who voted: 55.09

Popular vote for Bill Clinton: 44,909,326 (370 electoral votes)

Popular vote for George Bush: 39,103,882 (168 electoral votes)

Popular vote for Ross Perot: 19,741,657 (0 electoral votes)

Source: Federal Election Commission

CHAPTER THREE

Thinking About Tomorrow

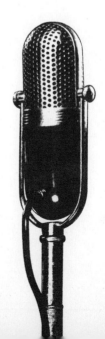

January 21, 1993. There's electricity everywhere in Washington, D.C., when America readies itself for Inauguration Day. Every four years bleachers go up along Constitution Avenue across from the White House so that VIPs can view the passing parade with its floats and marching bands from every state. For the non-VIP, one has to stake out a position along the parade route between the Capitol and the White House. But you know what? On Inauguration Day people aren't thinking about seating arrangements. It is the current in the air and the bunting that hangs from buildings. It is the street vendors hawking everything from license plates to ugly paintings of the new president to T-shirts. It is all right there in trailers and on banquet tables at ridiculously high prices to mark the arrival of the next White House occupant or at clearance sale prices to say goodbye to the present occupant. So if you can look beyond all the exteriors that define one way of seeing Inauguration Day, it is, like the election preceding it, about what is going on inside each of us. And it doesn't matter where you are seated.

I wasn't in the VIP section as the parade passed. I was in an office building with a huge balcony overlooking Constitution Avenue. The weather was crisp and the energy everyone was feeling seemed all the more intense because of a brilliant blue sky and bright sun. This was the perfect party; inside, a wide-screen TV (in 1993, fifty-two inches was wide-screen) carried the president's fourteen-minute inaugural address. Outside, I could see the people and actually hear Clinton's words echo through the streets. It was a few minutes later when Maya Angelou took to the podium and delivered a poem she had penned for this day called "On the Pulse of Morning." I felt the room change as she said the words and I knew it really wasn't the room but, rather, something inside me and a lot of other people.

That evening there were thirteen inaugural balls in Washington. I did my national radio show from the Four Seasons Hotel in Georgetown and it was, as usual when we go on the road, a wild fly-by-the-seat-of-your-pants experience. The place was packed and everywhere I could see what people were feeling. My first guest that night was Bill Clinton's chief of staff, Mack McLarty, who went to Miss Mary's kindergarten class in Hope, Arkansas, with the new president. He told me Clinton offered him the position the night after the election in a late meeting at the Governor's Mansion in Little Rock. McLarty wanted to think about it and, after a few weeks, agreed to take the position. And when I interviewed him inauguration night, he had already been on the job.

KING: Tell me what happened today after the
  inauguration. Did you go to work?
McLARTY: We did. I went to work this
  afternoon. We had people ready to answer
  the telephone at 12:01. I was at my desk by
  two.
KING: Are you looking forward to this?
McLARTY: There's a crosscurrent of emotions. I
  think that's natural. There's excitement, and
  it's an honor to serve people of this country
  and to work with a friend of forty years. But
  there's a certain amount of reflection and
  apprehension.
KING: Is the president going to continue to
  jog?
McLARTY: I think that's part of the way he
  keeps fit from a mental as well as a physical
  standpoint.

Art Buchwald and Mark Russell were up next, two men
who make their living from what happens, and doesn't happen, in Washington. Russell was going to be on stage at Ford's
Theater the following night, so I asked him to come up and
give us a preview. He sat next to me in his best deadpan
manner. Buchwald kept a straight face on my other side.

KING: Well, what's your sum-up of this first
  night, Mark?
RUSSELL: There was a moment of limbo,
  Larry, right at the swearing in. It was
  between the time that Gore was sworn in
  and the time Clinton was sworn in. Larry,

61

we had President Bush and Vice President
Gore!

KING: Are your hopes high, Art?

BUCHWALD: Larry, they were pretty low until
President Clinton as a candidate said he
had smoked marijuana but never inhaled.
And when I heard that I thought to myself
I can build a new tennis court on my
house.

KING: Mark, you see it that way?

RUSSELL: I really don't see what the big deal
is. The election laws are very clear and if
you had smoked marijuana here you just
have to wait until you get to England before
you exhale.

Judy Collins was the next guest and had just come from
one of the balls. The night before she had sung "Amazing
Grace" at the Capitol Center, which was taped for television. The Clintons were there and she told me he knew the
words to every song she sang that evening. It was a good
lead-in to the next question.

"What song," I asked, "do you think best describes this
day?"

She didn't miss a beat. "I've got sunshine, I've got blue
skies . . ." she began. The audience joined in and soon the
entire room was singing Gershwin's "I Got Rhythm." "That's
the song. That's what's going on tonight," she said to everyone. The crowd broke into applause. Everyone was feeling
the words that had spread throughout the day. They came
from Maya Angelou, certainly Gershwin, and to a lesser extent, Bill Clinton.

Before Bill Clinton had even taken the oath of office, stories quoting pundits and experts (two different animals) were to be found everywhere about what would, and wouldn't, be accomplished in the first hundred days. Indeed, Clinton brought most of this on himself during the campaign when he talked about education, health care, and the economy being on center stage before April 30 (the one hundredth day of his presidency). As much as I wanted to blame this preoccupation we seem to have with achievements of a fouryear term on only the first three and one third months as dumbing down, I knew the precedent lay with Franklin Roosevelt. He took office trying to show his critics and the public there was a well-thought-out game plan to get the country out of the Great Depression. And in those first hundred days, Roosevelt began fireside chats, declared a three-day national bank holiday so banks could be inspected for financial soundness, and began the Civilian Conservation Corps, which put a quarter of a million people to work. And that was just in the month of March. He framed the idea that the first hundred days were to be filled with accomplishment. They were just that but maybe more important was the symbolic gesture coming at a time when people were picking up the pieces. It offered hope.

But the idea of Doing Something in one hundred days had been a theme for Clinton. During the summer before the election he was telling anyone who would listen there would be an "explosive hundred-day action period." By mid-November he was talking about how he would "hit the ground running." But on the day before he was sworn in, Clinton's campaign strategist, James Carville, was telling audiences at the National Press Club to judge the president not on the first hundred days but, rather, the first four years, which sure made sense to me. Of course, when the lunch conversation at Duke Zeibert's wasn't about the usual topic—how to solve the problems of the world—it fell to the lowly idea of what could be done before April 30. Let me put it like this: On the former, we had solutions in place before the iced tea arrived. On the latter, nobody had a clue. Still, on Day 98 I had a conversation with New York governor Mario Cuomo and asked, "Hey, on a scale of 1 to 10, where do you place Bill Clinton?" Cuomo looked at me and asked a question right back: "Larry, how many days in a term?" I had no idea and I knew right away this was a question I shouldn't have gotten involved with. "Fourteen hundred sixty days in a term," he said. "You're asking about the first hundred of 1,460? This is two outs in the first inning." Sheepishly, I agreed, but just take a guess at what the topic of *Larry King Live* was on April 30?

In the last interview he had done with me before the election, which took place in Louisville, Clinton said he would come on *Larry King Live* every six months to discuss issues and take questions from viewers. I hadn't asked the essential follow-up question at the time about if the offer was good *if* he wins the election but he kept his word. Exactly six months after we had watched him become the forty-second president of the United States on that January afternoon, we sat together in the Library of the White House on a sultry July evening for another live show. We went on the air at 9:00 P.M. and he came into the room a little after eight for makeup. We took pictures with the staff and then had some time to just stand around shooting the breeze with each other. We looked out a window at the lights of the city and I sensed

Clinton taking a deep breath, sort of wistful, and so I had to ask a question.

"How do you feel when you look out there?"

The answer came right away. "You know, a lot of times I wish I could just go walking." He looked around the room we were in and pointed. "This is just so insulated. I mean it's heady but beyond that it's insulated." He looked right at me. "It's lonely."

"Well," I said, "you're the president now. It probably should be a little different than being in Little Rock."

Clinton was smiling. "Larry, when I was governor, I could go to shopping malls if I wanted." He looked out the window. "Not anymore."

I made the comment that I thought Elvis Presley lived a more isolated life than he did because it was self-imposed, rather than part of the job. He was going to respond when we were called to the set. It was show time. And within two minutes of going on the air, we were talking about, well, you know what.

CLINTON: It can be very isolating here.

KING: Do you have to fight it?

CLINTON: I fight it all the time. It can be isolating. There is so much to do that you have to be very disciplined about your time. And I think the more I'm in this office, the more I've become conscious of it and, I think, the more disciplined I've become about my time. But discipline means deciding things you won't do, people you won't see, calls you won't make.

65

The interview was going well and we touched on a lot of issues: He said gays should be in the military because "it ought to be conduct, not your orientation," he thought his nominee to replace Judge William Sessions at the FBI, Louie Freeh, was going to receive Senate confirmation, and he hoped Judge Ruth Bader Ginsburg would make it to the Supreme Court. And then there was NAFTA. He was going to go after votes for ratification, which was opposed by the most unique collection of folks I could imagine: Ross Perot, Jerry Brown, and Pat Buchanan. During the 9:30 commercial break, I leaned over and asked, "You want to keep going past ten?" He nodded and said, "Absolutely." So as we came back I announced to both CNN and the White House, as well as the international audience, that we were going for an extra half hour. I didn't notice, however, the conversation taking place off camera between David Gergen and George Stephanopoulos and Mack McLarty. Instead, I was focused on asking questions about what movies he watches and military base closings. We took calls from Montreal and the British Virgin Islands and I wondered, "Gee, what about the farm family in Nebraska or the autoworker in Lansing or the retired couple in Florida?" It seemed all the calls we went through were from outside the U.S.A. He answered each question at length and the next thing I knew we were up against another commercial break. As soon as I pitched to it, Stephanopoulos and McLarty were on the set. "Mr. President," the chief of staff said, "let's get off at ten." As this is going on I'm sitting there watching and thinking to myself, "Hey, he's the president of the United States and he oughta be able to decide if he wants to sit for another thirty minutes or not and, what the hell, it's late at night and, as far as I can tell, he's got nothing else to do even if he is the president." I didn't offer this cogent observation. I looked again at Clinton and it was clear he was upset.

"Why would I want to do that?" he snapped. "You don't think I'm doing good enough to stay until 10:30? Is that it? You think something's going to happen?"

By this time even I could tell something was going on. McLarty took a deep breath but stayed focused on his kindergarten chum. It was pretty clear President Clinton wasn't going to do an extra thirty minutes.

"Please, Mr. President," he pleaded. "Leave at ten."

I had never seen Bill Clinton ticked. No question about it. He glared at McLarty. "Are you telling me to keep count of the good things and not risk a bad one?" He shook his head as the floor director started counting me into the next segment. As this happened, the producer in my headset said we were definitely out at ten and I'd be filled in after the show. In this business, you don't argue the point with two seconds to air.

"We're back on *Larry King Live*," I said. "The president had another commitment he didn't know about, so there's a schedule conflict. He'll be with us to the top of the hour." I figured it this way: He owed me. And so I decided to hold him to it in front of the world.

"However, we have a rotating date every six months, right, as promised during the campaign."

Clinton looked right at me. There was no smile anymore. "I owe you a half hour now," he said.

"So the next appearance will be ninety minutes." See, I had an hour coming and he was in to me for another half. You gotta always know the score.

"You bet."

"Or two hours." Producers in Atlanta now were saying it

in my headset and so I was the middle man in a negotiation with the president of the United States. "Atlanta is pointing out two hours. They never stop. Two hours? Okay? But there was another appointment he was unaware of and we were unaware of."

We talked about NAFTA and then went to another phone call, this one from Paris. Now even I knew there was something going on. Something had happened and only Clinton and Larry were the ones without a clue. We hit the last commercial break and I made small talk with him. He leaned into my ear and said, "As soon as we're off the air I'm going to find out what the hell this is. We'll have some coffee." CNN in Atlanta and Washington is hearing all this and I could hear my producer calmly say, "We'll explain, Larry. We'll explain."

The last phone call was about Clinton's legacy. It was a good question.

"Is it too early to have a legacy?" I asked. I knew the answer. "Well, Larry," he would say, "I have so much to do right now it just isn't possible for me to think about what will be said after I leave." That's what I was expecting to hear. Wrong again.

"I'd be happy to tell you that," he began. "Number one, I'd like to get the economy moving again. Number two, I'd like to provide health security for all Americans. Number three, I want my national service plan to pass. It will open doors of college education to millions of Americans for lower interest loans and give many, many of them the chance to work those loans off through service to their communities. Number four, I strongly want to pass a welfare reform bill that will move people from welfare to work and end welfare

as we know it. And five, I want to reform the political system. I'd like those things in my legacy."

I was flat-out amazed. The guy had been in office for six
months and he was able to rattle off what he wanted the historians to write. It was clear this wasn't any ad lib. Bill Clinton had given a lot of thought to the question.

As soon as I said "good night," Stephanopoulos and
McLarty grabbed Clinton by the arm as he was taking out
his earpiece, which is used to hear the phone calls. They
whispered something to him and everyone was out of the
room like a bat out of hell. Me? I sat there thinking I'm going
to get invited somewhere for coffee. And that's when I got
a phone call from the Washington bureau. Bill Clinton's lifelong friend and special assistant for legal affairs, Vince Foster, had been found dead in Fort Marcy Park just off the
George Washington Parkway overlooking the Potomac River.
Preliminary reports were that he had killed himself. The
White House was worried, and rightfully so, that someone
might hear the news on a police scanner and then call in to
ask the president about it on the air. They didn't want him
to find out about it that way, which was why no domestic
phone calls were taken.

Soon it was learned that White House aides had gone
into Vince Foster's office and removed files. At the same
time, attempts by federal investigators to search the office for
possible clues immediately following the death as to why Foster might have killed himself were rebuffed by the White
House. This started the whispers which started the supposition which started the conspiracy theories which started the
wackos or, now that I think about it, the wackos started on
their own and were probably in motion before Foster had
even gotten into the White House. The frenzy was off and

69

running. Supposition was in full swing and being driven by a determined anger I'd never seen before or heard. It was mean-spirited and it became a topic at lunch. I thought it was the result of so many television channels having to vamp for time and using talking heads offering opinions based on no facts whatsoever as well as the right-wing talk radio programs, which, after a while, started to sound like echo chambers. Now, all you would hear was "ditto" or "me-too" or the constant use of the words "we" and "they" as if some kind of armed conflict was at hand. The conclusion at lunch in that first week after the death was there are a lot of people who hate Bill Clinton. The White House was always putting that kind of spin on stories when things didn't work out for the administration, which was probably true 60 percent of the time. This was the first time I really sensed the dislike that was out there. And today when we gather for lunch, that initial idea hasn't changed.

But certainly, the Vince Foster death was reason to wonder if there was a connection between something occurring in the White House and what occurred in that little park. That was legitimate. Everything after that was speculation. And I knew it would still be a topic ten years later whether there was a formal conclusion or not. These were the times we were in.

In 1961 I had gone to then mayor of Miami Elliot Roosevelt and asked if he could do me a favor. It wasn't getting a traffic ticket fixed because I never bothered the mayor with seemingly minor issues like that (usually a circuit court judge could get the job done). I knew his mother, Eleanor, would visit from time to time and I asked that he be the go-between to have her come on my talk show at WIOD Radio. Elliot came through and, at age twenty-three, I had the chance to spend an hour with the former first lady talking about her book, *Autobiography* (my show was new so I wasn't exactly on the stopping-off list for every celebrity that came to town).

Thirty-one years later I had the chance to talk about my time with Eleanor while sitting in the White House with the current first lady. Hillary Rodham Clinton and I were taping the first show of *Larry King Weekend*. We spent a few moments talking about a woman for whom, I was soon to learn, she had great respect. Mrs. Clinton had been compared to Eleanor within the first few minutes of the new administration as she was asked to chair a Health Care Task Force with presidential advisor Ira Magaziner taking charge of day-to-day operations. And it was part of the hundred-day plan at the White House: deliver a health care package that was backed by the people and with the ability to get through Congress.

Mrs. Roosevelt had told me serving in public office was good for one's ideals but very high in personal sacrifice. I didn't know it at the time but she said that back in the 1940s and had, simply, repeated it to me during the interview. As a result, I was always quick to point out when telling this story that it was nothing new. Mrs. Clinton had heard the line and I think she identified with the thought her predecessor had so many years earlier. But then, I'm sure Martha Washington was thinking the same thing. In fact, Nancy Reagan had said to me, "Nothing can prepare you for the White House." Eleanor Roosevelt had told me it was common for the president to bounce ideas off her before talking to anyone else because if she didn't understand what he was saying, nobody else was going to understand either. That street went two ways.

KING: She always felt that Franklin, as she
called him, deserved her opinion and had to
hear it. Whether she carried the day or not,
when she disagreed, he should hear it. Does
Hillary Clinton feel the same?

CLINTON: I agree with that. I think there are
many things I don't have an opinion about
that my husband deals with every day, but
there are some things I have a strong
opinion about, and if he asks me or if I feel
very strongly about it, like most wives that I
know, I will share it with him.

Just a week earlier Mrs. Clinton had testified before a
House subcommittee on her role as chairperson of the Health
Care Task Force. Begun less than a month after the Clinton
administration had come to town, the project was under fire
from the get-go. The task force had traveled around the country to get opinions from health care experts as well as pa-
tients, which was a good idea, even a necessary idea, but the
meetings weren't open to the public. Within a month of the
first meeting Hillary and the task force were sued. And on
the hundredth day, Mrs. Clinton met with senators from both
sides of the aisle in an attempt to find out what she was
doing wrong. One month later, the task force went out of
business.

I didn't have a chance to talk with Hillary for another
six months, but she made good on a promise to come into
the studio and take phone calls. And that's where she talked
to me about anger, which, she said, was part of the reason
the first attempt at a health care program had fallen flat.

CLINTON: I think some of it is because I'm a
kind of transition person in the history of
the country.

KING: Meaning what?

CLINTON: The life I've led, trying to balance
family and work, is what we're all trying to
work out in our own lives. But we've never
had somebody in my position before who
had done that.

Transition is always the toughest. And when you have
partisan politics (which is nothing new) combined with the
never-ending banter from multiple channels (which is new)
and toss that into the pot called "these times" (also new),
well, transition becomes all the tougher. The Clinton administration was having a tough time not only with health
care, but also with the NAFTA trade pact. President Bush
had worked to put the pieces together during his term when
he signed the comprehensive treaty agreement with Canada.
And he had signed the agreement with Mexico that October afternoon before I interviewed him in San Antonio. Now
President Clinton had to carry it over the line. Actually two
lines; first the House, and then the Senate. But there was
another line too; it belonged to a collection of opponents
never before in agreement on anything. Ross Perot hated the
idea of NAFTA and started talking about the "giant sucking
sound" as businesses and jobs left America if trade barriers
were lowered. It was The Topic and the White House was
thirty votes short in the House, where it was scheduled for
a vote in November. One morning my phone rang.

"Larry, it's Al." The voice was friendly.

"Al who?" I didn't know anyone named Al.

"Al, Larry. Al Gore. Look, I'll debate Perot. I'll do it on your show." He didn't even have to tell me the topic. Like I said, it was The Topic.

I had talked to Al Gore off and on for years when he was a senator from Tennessee. I can remember him calling me to suggest I interview particular authors on the radio show. I don't think I ever followed through with his suggestions but this was one I thought would be a good show.

"Larry, you there?"

"Sure," I said. I just couldn't say "Mr. Vice President."

"Can you set it up?"

"I'll go to work on it today," I said.

"You think he'll do it? He can name the time and place."

"I'll make some calls and let you know."

We hung up and within ten seconds I was talking to my new senior executive producer Wendy Walker Whitworth at *Larry King Live*. I called Ross, who immediately said the words "fine with me." Wendy worked out November 9 as the date in the CNN Washington studio.

It had been less than a week since the call from Gore. That night Ross Perot showed up with more people than I'd ever seen him with since he started appearing on the show: one other guy. Gore was there with George Stephanopoulos, David Gergen, and James Carville (yeah, Carville wore jeans). Bill Clinton stayed at the White House to watch it there.

The only ground rules were that no advisors could come into the studio during commercial breaks. Once we started, each was on his own. In fact, other than the three of us, only the makeup person could go onto the set. We were two minutes away from the start when Gore walked away and rested his arm on top of one of the cameras. He was quiet for a moment but I do remember watching him take a deep breath. He was facing away from us and by now both Ross and I were watching. We looked at each other and shrugged our shoulders. Gore came back and sat down and shook hands with Ross. We posed for a few quick pictures. At 9:00 P.M. straight up, history began on *Larry King Live*. You never think about history before it happens. I didn't say to anyone during lunch at Duke's that day, "Hey, watch tonight because we're gonna make history." It just shows up and, as always, without fanfare.

Both Gore and Perot had pictures with them. Perot had a photo of a Mexican living in a cardboard box that once contained U.S. products shipped to Mexico. The standard of living for Mexican workers continues to go down, he said, and Gore started asking how Perot would change the situation. Perot said he would go back and study the issue.

> GORE: How would you change it? What
> specific changes would you make?
> PEROT: I can't unless you let me finish, I can't
> answer your question. Now you asked me
> and I'm trying to tell you.
> GORE: Well you brought your charts tonight so
> I want to know what specific changes you
> would make in the treaty.
> KING: That's a fair question. Let him respond,
> okay?
> PEROT: How can I respond if you keep
> interrupting me?

This happened ten times during the hour and a half. And I think it hurt Ross. Perot had the photograph of the poor Mexican. Gore had a photograph of two members of Congress named Smoot and Hawley who sponsored, get ready, the Smoot-Hawley Protection Bill in 1930, which raised tariffs on U.S. products to protect workers. Gore said Smoot-Hawley could be linked to the Great Depression. Gore then handed the framed photograph to Perot and suggested Ross's position was similar to theirs. During breaks I spent most of my time trying to cool them down. Toward the end of the show, however, I sensed I was coming close to losing control.

> CALLER: The subject has come up about the Japanese taking over if NAFTA doesn't go through. I'm American. I've been living in Mexico City for many years. There are thousands of Japanese here. They are waiting. They are lurking. What are you people doing? (Caller was disconnected.)
>
> GORE: Let me answer that.
>
> PEROT: Does he get to answer first every time?
>
> KING: I think the question was for him.
>
> GORE: You go ahead and answer it.
>
> PEROT: No, you go ahead.
>
> GORE: I'd like to answer but you go ahead first.

All the time I'm thinking, "This is crazy." But we got through the ninety minutes and I knew it was good. The tension between them was good as much as it was bad. There was a drama to what could have been an academic argument. Let me put it this way: Not too many American families sit around their television at night to watch a program about trade agreements. That night, more than 11 million people tuned in. AT&T said more calls from out of the country had been dialed to CNN than at any other time in history. It was the highest-rated program in cable history at that time. Now of course that says something about the participants. But more important was the fact people watched it because they cared about the issue. We were into new territory now. Congressional offices were deluged with phone calls as a result of that show. And if television hadn't played a role in politics before November 9, it certainly played a role in how votes were cast eight days later in the House as NAFTA passed 234–200. Three days after that, the Senate approved it on a 61–38 vote.

It had been Ross Perot who told me that issues in the future would be debated in an electronic town hall. Indeed, voters could watch the points being argued, make their decision as to what side they prefer, and either vote on issues themselves (in the case of a presidential race) or let their congressman or senator know how a vote should be taken. And in a small way, that's exactly what we did for ninety minutes. Ross was right on the money.

As soon as the show was over both Gore and Perot shook hands. The vice president slapped me on the back and walked off the set. I didn't have a chance to ask him about what he did next to that camera an hour and a half earlier until years had passed. "I said a prayer," he told me. He knew this was a big moment and probably the biggest moment of his national and international career.

I later learned the White House was against the idea. But Gore argued the point saying he had all the facts. Clinton listened to this and then offered to debate Perot himself. He was told a sitting president debating a private citizen wasn't presidential. He had to be talked into letting Gore do it.

Ross meanwhile thought he had won the debate. I think that's why he's such a good salesman. After Gore had walked out of the studio Ross looked at me and asked if I had noticed that Gore's earpiece, which is used to hear telephone calls, was different from the one he used. I told him Gore had a special one that is custom-made for his ear because he does so many interview programs. I have one too and I showed him mine while making the suggestion he get one too. Ross looked at it but wasn't buying my explanation. "The thing in Gore's ear looked different, Larry. I think he was plugged into the White House. I think they were feeding him answers." I listened and thought Ross was putting me on. He wasn't. "Larry, they had a direct funnel to Gore."

"That's not it at all," I said, having no clue what I was talking about because I'm not any kind of expert on earplugs or microphones or any of the other things that are always on the set. "Gore heard nothing different from what you or I heard."

He got up to leave. "Well, can you swear to me it isn't?"

"I swear to it." We shook hands and he smiled and he was gone. I sat there on the set for a moment wondering if maybe Ross *was* joking with me.

The next night I went to a party for Senator Lloyd Bentsen that was attended by Bill Clinton. I walked over and said hello and he shook my hand. "Larry, I owe you big time," he said. "We changed the world last night."

On December 8, NAFTA was signed into law. I wasn't paying a lot of attention to it because I was trying to replace batteries in the most important invention of the twentieth century and not having a lot of luck doing it. Just as I had decided the hell with it and I'd just buy a new TV clicker, the "breaking news" graphic came on. I looked up to see President Clinton in the Mellon Auditorium and half listened as he started speaking about this being an historic day. Then he stopped reading from his prepared remarks.

> I also can't help but note that in spite of all the rest
> of our efforts, there was a magic moment on Larry
> King which made a lot of difference. And I thank the
> vice president for that and for so much else.

Suddenly, the remote control just didn't seem important (I sure didn't want to change the channel). I sat there on the sofa as the batteries fell between the cushions and wondered if Clinton was right; that we had changed the world that night. And I didn't know if I liked the idea of a television show having that kind of ability. But then I took it one step further: What is anyone going to do about it? Are we gonna say don't broadcast this or that because a change in society is a possibility? And is the burden on television or is it on the viewer? I had an answer. The question was moot. It had happened and will probably happen again.

A few hours later I walked into Duke Zeibert's and took a seat in Siberia because Jack Kent Cooke was holding court at his table. Duke walked over as I sipped coffee and shook his head.

"What?" I asked.

"Larry, you made the second paragraph today at the White House," Duke told me.

"Yeah, that was pretty good, huh?" I offered. Duke shook his head again.

"No, I don't think so," he said. "See if you can get into the first paragraph the next time." He smiled and started working the room as only Duke can do. I finished lunch all

79

the time wondering if getting into the first paragraph might get me out of Siberia.

That Christmas I was invited to the White House for a few hours of food and conversation along with about five hundred other members of the media. It is an opportunity to walk through a number of the rooms just off the East Room (that's where prime-time news conferences were held back in the days when people watched prime-time news conferences) and see the incredible decorations that are a part of America's House. That Christmas party brought back memories from Ocala and Louisville during the campaign. I watched both President and Mrs. Clinton greet each person with a smile, take their hands and have a conversation, and then pose for a picture. They had been doing this for an hour before I even got to the White House and they were still at it when I left to go to work on the radio show. I remember Clinton's Santa Claus tie and my thought at the time was "I wonder if he was wearing that while dealing with Yeltsin?" To me, that would be the definition of an ability to compartmentalize, which is what people who knew Clinton were always saying about him.

And a month later he was sitting with me in the White House, ready to roll for ninety minutes as we had negotiated on air during the last interview. Clinton had gone through a number of rough days: his mother had died, he had a European trip scheduled, his choice for secretary of defense, Bobby Inman, had decided against taking the job, and on the same day he returned from Europe, an earthquake rocked Los Angeles. Clinton got back on *Air Force One* and went to the scene and then came back to Washington.

He was whipped. I could tell by his first answer. I had

asked him to look back and tell me what was the biggest surprise after one year in office.

> There was in this city, a culture that I knew existed
> that tended to sometimes major in the minors and
> minor in the majors, but I still found that if we
> stayed after it, we could change things. It just turned
> out to be harder than I thought it would be.

As we did this interview, Whitewater was becoming more of an issue with every new day. Quite frankly, it was beyond me. The Clintons had invested in a 230-acre land deal along the White River in Arkansas and it was a colossal failure. They lost money. And now Congress was making noises about investigating, which meant more money would be spent looking into what happened than was lost in the first place. In fact, Whitewater had been a conversation for exactly sixty seconds at lunch one afternoon and all assembled agreed we just didn't care about a money-losing venture fifteen years earlier, even if the Clintons had done something wrong. "You just can't keep on about everything the guy did because you end up spending more time worrying about where he was than where he is," I said to the table. Heads nodded in agreement, or maybe because nobody cared enough to disagree, but that was the extent of my discussions on Whitewater when I wasn't working.

However, on the evening I was sitting with the president, Attorney General Janet Reno had named former U.S. Attorney Robert Fiske to be the special prosecutor for Whitewater. Fiske announced he was also going to investigate whether or not there was a link between Vince Foster's suicide and his knowledge of Whitewater. Looking back on this

81

moment, I realize it was the first time we heard the president speak about wanting to go back to work for the American people, or a variation on that theme, when the heat was starting to increase.

About a month later I was interviewing James McDougal, the financial partner with whom the Clintons were involved on the Whitewater project. As the interview began I explained to the audience that tonight's program deals with Whitewater and if anyone knew about the topic then it would be my guest. As I'm speaking I noticed McDougal holding a plastic bag in his hand and my first impression was the guy had something illegal. The second impression was why would he bring something illegal here? See, it's possible to look at a camera and sound convincing while your mind is elsewhere.

> McDOUGAL: There's been a great deal of
> searching. I think we've had more than two
> hundred members of the press corps in
> Little Rock from various media groups
> looking for dirt from Whitewater. So, I have
> brought you the only genuine dirt I can
> guarantee, and that is ownership of one
> square foot of Whitewater.
>
> KING: I'm honored.
>
> McDOUGAL: Anyone else who desires to own
> it can have the same by sending $20 to our
> defense fund.

Let me tell you something: I still have the dirt. And when I was leaving the studio that evening, one of the crew offered to take it off my hands. "Absolutely not," I said. And it was the topic at lunch the next day.

"So tell me, Larry," asked my boyhood friend from Brooklyn Herb Cohen, "what did you do with the Whitewater land you now own?"

"Don't worry about it," I said. "I'm taking care of it."

"Could probably bring some good bucks at an auction for your charity," he said. I knew where he was going with this. Start the guilt trip. Here are two grown guys playing games over dirt.

"Send McDougal $20 and get your own."

Herb looked at me. "You're serious. You are going to keep that dirt?"

"I have dirt from Ebbetts Field and right next to it is the dirt from Whitewater." Herb wasn't getting any of it, be it my point or my dirt. The conversation stopped for a while as we finished lunch. When I got up to leave the table, he looked me in the eye and said with a straight face, "Just make sure you don't mix any of it up with the other because that will just kill the value." When I got to my car my mind was made up. The two dirts would be kept in separate closets. They still are.

Speaking of which, Congress wanted to investigate whether or not there was any dirt (the other kind of dirt, not what I had) in Whitewater. I knew it was a pursuit of the truth but I also knew the search included a member of Congress reading a statement while a witness patiently waited for a question to be asked. I knew it would become a show, despite how much we would hear about the exercise being an attempt to out what really happened. I also didn't see any reason for Congress to investigate when there was already a special prosecutor assigned to the matter. This meant there would be hearings, which meant we'd have a debate about whether or not to televise the hearings, and I knew when

83

the day was done that CNN would be covering the witnesses and cross-examination. It's a dilemma and we're never going to be able to hold any kind of televised Congressional hearing without the possibility of grandstanding, be it from Congress or a witness before Congress. And I knew one other thing: If Americans weren't talking about Whitewater over lunch, they sure weren't going to talk about it after eight hours or eight months on TV because nobody would be interested enough to watch.

The greatest deliberative body, as it's called, deliberated another five months before the Whitewater hearings began in the Senate. The president and first lady testified in separate sessions in the Treaty Room at the White House during the summer. And the special prosecutor was thrown out by an appeals court because he was appointed by Attorney General Reno and that was considered a conflict of interest. He was replaced by some guy, a former judge named Ken Starr.

I left the radio show in May 1994 after thirty-seven years in the business. There were two reasons: For the first time in my life, I didn't need the money and, second, because television is so demanding on not only one's time but one's soul. CNN wanted me to travel to Asia for interviews relating to Hong Kong no longer being controlled by British rule. They also wanted me in Normandy to mark the fiftieth anniversary of the landing at Omaha Beach. Now, radio can originate just as easily from all of these places but it would mean competition for guests in one place on one topic and I'd be working all night long or all morning long or parts of both because of time zone differences and I just didn't want to complicate a life that was already too complicated.

We did a show from the American Cemetery at Colevillesur-Mer in Normandy and had, among the guests, a German tank commander along with an American who had been in the third wave to come ashore on D-Day. They were in separate segments of the show, but it was clear the American wasn't pleased to be in the same place with the German. And he told me so on the air. But we did have a good conversation about where he was fifty years earlier and he told me this was a topic he didn't get into very often. I always thought it was good psychology to talk about experiences, but that was a day when I learned it's not that people don't want to talk about this, it's that they can't. And then there was a call we took from Duluth, Minnesota, which taught me something about what I've been doing for the past thirty-seven years:

> I've been taping since three yesterday afternoon, and
> I have cried so many times. I have never heard most
> of what I've seen, you know? You read in history
> books, but it doesn't even compare to seeing these
> men cry and retell their stories.

When we were driving back to the hotel after doing that show, someone in the car said, "You know, this is the way I wish I could have taken high school history. Forget the books and just let me watch people who were there tell the story." I didn't say anything. I was trying to remember the name of my history teacher.

On the first day back to work from the trip to France the big story was threats made by North Korea about banning weapons inspections. Adding to the heat, North Korea made it clear that any sanctions imposed by the United States (or anyone else, but we all know who was going to get involved) would be considered an act of war. This was, as George Bush's national security advisor, Brent Scowcroft, told me on the air that evening, "a prime-time crisis." Former President Carter was in Seoul trying to mediate the dispute and I was feeling pretty pessimistic about how this was going to turn out.

There was another story from that day. O.J. Simpson's ex-wife had been found murdered on the sidewalk in front of her home. Next to her body was that of a waiter named Ronald Goldman. O.J. had been in Chicago and returned to Los Angeles after being contacted by police. Before going on the air with the Korea story I had been briefed by the producers that we may have to pitch to a news conference with an update on the O.J. story. I wasn't going to argue because I knew if a story involves someone well known, it becomes an even larger story. But I kept saying to myself, "Holy shit, not O.J." Three months earlier I had been in Miami as master of ceremonies for a Don Shula golf tournament dinner and presented O.J. with the first-place trophy. And now this. Within a few minutes of taking air, we went live to Commander David Gascon of the L.A. Police Department, who proceeded to outline how the investigation into the two murders was going to be handled. I knew one other thing: While it was a major homicide case, it was going to be a two-, maybe three-day story and then it would be over with.

CHAPTER FOUR

A Mirror on the Screen

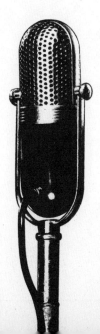

June 1994. I knew I was wrong about O.J. exactly two minutes after the North Korea show came to a close. I had done the hour with Brent Scowcroft thinking it was a newsmaker and that we had brought the viewer close to the story through the words of people who are on the front lines. North Korea was making noise in an area already unstable and South Korea's most populous center was just twenty-five miles from the border. It had the potential of being a real mess.

As I left the studio, though, I looked at the monitor as the anchor in Atlanta did the lead story. The story was O.J. I stood and watched and listened. So did the rest of the crew. I knew now what the topic was going to be on the next show.

It was also the topic at lunch the next day. In fact, I'll lay odds it was the topic at every lunch taking place in America. "It's a miniseries," my boyhood buddy from Brooklyn Herb Cohen announced. "You got the money, you got the hero, you got the horrible murder. We see this on TV every night and in every movie." He was right. As we spoke, helicopters were hovered over O.J.'s Rockingham Drive home and hundreds of reporters were on the street. I had driven to lunch at Duke's that day listening to the all-news station instead of "How High the Moon" on the big-band station. I wanted to hear O.J. come out and say "I didn't do it" or hear the Los Angeles police call a last-minute news conference to announce an apprehension had been made. Like all of us, I wanted the good guy to win and the bad guy to be led away and the whole story buttoned up within a set amount of time. It made me wonder if the way it works on TV or in the movies is how we start to expect the chaos of every day to operate. On one level I knew it to be ridiculous. On another, I kept listening to the radio expecting to hear the bulletin that it was over.

It didn't happen. By Friday, though, something else happened. O.J. had made arrangements to surrender to L.A. police. He didn't; at least not right away. Instead, he left a suicide note and disappeared. And by the time I went on the air at 9:00 P.M. that night, O.J. was still missing. The suicide note had been read by his close friend Robert Kardashian. The words made all of us in the studio shiver when they were played as a "bump," the video insert going into and coming out of commercials that we used every evening.

> I can't go on. No matter what the outcome, people
> will look and point. I can't take that. I can't subject
> my children to that. This way they can move on and
> go on with their lives. Please, if I have done anything
> worthwhile, let my kids live in peace from you, the
> press.

I had watched movies and TV shows with suicide notes. They were usually one page because the audience gets bored if it goes on too long. I sat there in the Washington studio watching the commercial bump, realizing this was very very real. And very uncomfortable. My guests were jury consultant Jo-Ellan Dimitrius and criminal defense attorney Barry Tarlow.

> KING: Jo-Ellan, has the press overdone it?
> DIMITRIUS: Well it would certainly seem that
> way with the consumption of information
> that's been out there. Generally, people
> believe that, you know 80 percent if there's
> an arrest, where there's smoke there's fire.
> And I think that the isolation of this one
> incident, in terms of world news, has just
> been so overwhelming and I think,
> obviously, has affected O.J. to the point
> where certainly, as a result of that letter, it
> sounds as though he's considering taking his
> own life, if he hasn't already.

Her last line got me. I knew I had to ask a question to Barry Tarlow but the idea that O.J. might be dead as we sat in the studio was something I just hadn't considered. But then there were probably movies or TV shows where the suicide note was actually a confession. I didn't know what category it belonged in because (1) this was something that probably required some reflection rather than an instant analysis and (2) I was too busy doing my job, which had as a base, many times, instant analysis. Today, with a few years to reflect and have lunch over it, those words were a sad confession of sorts. Do I have proof? Nope. Just a gut feeling and it took this long to even have a gut feeling.

> KING: Barry, too much?
> TARLOW: Absolutely. I understand that the
> public has a right to know and journalists
> have a right to do something. But there
> must be something more important in the
> world going on. You have 200 people from
> the press camped out on Rockingham Drive
> in Brentwood watching his house. I mean,
> they're accomplishing nothing.

During the hour the police were looking for O.J., the reporters were looking at them as they searched. Then it changed. The air monitor changed to a highway scene just as a voice in my ear from the control room said, "They have O.J in the white Bronco and that's a live feed." I started talking as I looked at the shot from a helicopter over a Los Angeles freeway. We brought up the audio feed of the KCAL reporter who was saying the police chase was taking place right now on Highway 5. In 1994 I hadn't spent a lot of time in Los Angeles other than going from LAX (the airport) to the Beverly Wilshire and then to the CNN Sunset Boulevard studio, so I was flying with the story not knowing where or when or if it would land. CNN producer Rick Davis was watching all of this from the control room and had the foresight to know Larry was live in front of millions of people without a clue of Los Angeles streets and handed me a road map while the air monitor showed the police chase. I found I-5 and put a finger on the area. I kept thinking how quickly my needs were changing during this show: First I was hoping O.J to be alive and not follow through with the words in the letter, and now I was wishing I knew which way on I-5 he was headed.

The chase went into the next hour and I stayed with it. And then it went into another hour. All the networks were carrying the chase. But NBC had a real dilemma because it had the New York Knicks–Houston Rockets NBA championship game. On one hand you have the rabid basketball fans camped in front of their sets and then you have this major story complete with great video. The network chose to jump from one story to the next, which, I can only guess, was an attempt to avoid another *Heidi* (In 1968, NBC pulled out of the Jets–Raiders game at the top of the hour because it had scheduled the classic *Heidi* to run at that moment. Football fans weren't happy. Many are still ticked. Of course, as this was going on I wasn't really watching NBC, although I was rooting for the Knicks), but one wonders why they couldn't have just done a split screen so both camps could be kept happy. I have a feeling the clickers that were aimed at NBC started being put to work along with the required four-letter words.

The white Bronco, with O.J.'s longtime friend Al Cowlings at the wheel, ended up at Simpson's house and, after O.J. made a call to his mother and talked to his attorney, he went to the Los Angeles County jail. This was unlike any other show I'd done because at no time was I ever in control of events. I hadn't a clue what route the white Bronco was going to take, I didn't know (for a while anyway) if O.J. was even in the white Bronco, and it was a story happening right in front of everyone. It was a miniseries and nobody knew the ending, not even O.J., I would venture to guess.

When I got off the air three hours later, I was absolutely

whipped. I didn't stick around to talk about it other than to ask if the Knicks won. Nobody knew. Nobody cared. Everyone else was tired too. We all just walked to our cars in silence thinking through what we had just seen rather than what we had all just done. Driving home I turned on all-news WTOP to hear the Knicks score but they were talking about, well, you know what they were talking about. By the time I got in my door, I didn't care who had won (for the record, Houston took the series in seven games, so it doesn't really matter who won this one).

The next morning my ex-wife Sharon called me to say she had been on the last flight from Atlanta to Washington and the gate crew was having trouble boarding passengers because so many wanted to see as much of the chase as possible on the airport television monitors before getting on the plane. Normally 50 million people watch television on a Friday night in America. "The chase," as it came to be called, brought the number to 75 million. CNN hadn't had a night this good since NAFTA. But the big news to me was the fact that for the first time since we had learned about this late Sunday night, the *New York Times* had put the O.J. story on the front page instead of burying it inside somewhere. Yeah, the media, whatever the media is, was playing a role not only in what we saw and read and heard, but it was a subject we now automatically talked about. And I'm still not sure if that's good or bad or just plain moot.

I took the Metroliner to New York that morning and ended up in a brief conversation with a beautiful lady who refused, despite my efforts, to give me her name. She was making a weekly trip to Manhattan to have nails and hair done and do some shopping. Our conversation started with the *New York Times*. Well, okay, I started the conversation. For the record, folks, I was single.

"They have admitted it's a story," I said to her while pointing to the below-the-fold placement.

"I'm surprised you were able to get this early a train," she said. "You were busy last night."

"Thank you for watching," I answered, getting ready to move across the aisle to where she was sitting. That was exactly the moment she pulled her carryon bag off the floor and into the seat I was headed for. I've been around and I pick up on these things real quick. So I went back to the newspaper that prints "all the news (and sometimes on the front page)."

"The thing I don't get is why I have to be told what an attorney should be doing or whether reporters are doing too much."

She was talking to me. But the damn bag hadn't moved.

"Just tell me the story," she went on. "I don't want all the inside stuff. I don't care." She had blue eyes. And her blond hair was pulled back. There was potential here.

"Everything is too much," I said, "but what is just enough?"

She looked at me. It wasn't one of those eyes-into-the-sky things when a person is looking for an answer. She was looking right at me. "I don't know the answer."

I looked at her and I wasn't thinking the way I usually think in this kind of a situation. "You know something," I said, "I don't know the answer either." For the rest of the train ride we were both absorbed in our books and newspapers. When you don't have answers, there's not much to say unless, of course, you're on a TV program.

Over the next few weeks the owner of a Los Angeles knife shop told the court he had sold a knife to O.J. And then he sold the story to the *National Enquirer* for $12,000. Meanwhile Kato Kaelin, O.J.'s famous house guest, had been offered a quarter of a million dollars to talk to the *Enquirer* and turned it down. So the topic the beautiful woman had complained to me about was now something into which we were going to go full blast. And it was fueled by the fact that *The New Yorker* had run an article by Jeffrey Toobin called "Cash for Trash." We brought Toobin into the studio along with the always lively national editor of the *Enquirer*, Mike Walker. His paper had a $1 million offer on the table to Al Cowlings, who had driven O.J. in the white Bronco. It was a show people still talk to me about because one had the feeling the guests were going to go after each other during each commercial break, if not while we were on the air.

> WALKER: We're unabashed about it. But we
> wouldn't let Al Cowlings say anything he
> wanted. We would check everything he said
> against known sources . . . we don't want to
> be wrong.
> KING: What do you make of that, Jeffrey?
> TOOBIN: It's more phony baloney nonsense.

When we were done, I thanked them all on camera and, one more time, off camera. Both Toobin and Walker were quiet now and I remember saying to the floor director they were probably going out for a beer together. And there's one other thing I remember from that interview. The beautiful lady on the train had better face the fact that everything once considered "inside" is now open for general discussion. We were going to talk about strategies by both the defense and prosecuting attorneys as well as how the police are doing their investigation and, of course, how it is all being covered by those with media credentials. I say this only because now I believed it too.

One thing O.J. had done was to keep problems Bill Clinton was having on health care and relations with Congress off the front page and the television and radio lead story and out of the lunch conversations (the only exception to this glittering generality was Washington, where the conversation still began with O.J., but the next sentence was something like "I hear Dole is gonna hold up anyone from talking to the White House about issues until the November election"). And nobody was talking about North Korea.

This changed for a few moments on July 21 when a judge ruled Paula Jones couldn't sue President Clinton as long as he was a sitting president. Jones was the Arkansas Industrial Development Commission employee who claimed in 1991, while working at a conference in Little Rock's Excelsior Hotel, then-Governor Clinton invited her up to a hotel room where he asked her to perform oral sex on him. She says she refused his offer and proceeded to file a $700,000 lawsuit seeking damages for "willful, outrageous, and malicious conduct," albeit after he became president. We had been through Gennifer Flowers and there were a lot of reports about "other women" leading up to, during, and after his election. I knew the first reference to "Paula" came in *The American Spectator* more than half a year earlier. And I was dubious because the magazine is so right wing that this just seemed to be one more attempt to derail Clinton. It was the classic he said–she said and, as a result, it came down to which of the two that were directly involved do you believe? I kept an open mind during the resulting frenzy and took neither side. But one thing I knew for certain was if Bill Clinton had been reckless in Arkansas, he sure couldn't be following the same path in Washington. Oh boy.

Of course this was another gift for the part-time Clinton opposition on the Hill and across America as well as the full-time opposition found in the listenership of Rush Limbaugh or Bob Grant or other radio talk show hosts who were collectively "outraged" or "shocked and appalled" by the governor's apparent misguided moral compass. And they ran with it, as well they should have. It was grist for the mill. Did America, by electing a man with a trail of alleged liaisons, condone this kind of behavior? And by the actions of this judge, what kind of message are we sending to families in America? Each host had the same level of anger as they asked the question trying to rally the troops, who were great at picking up the phone and bitching. I had always wondered, setting aside First Amendment arguments, what would happen if you could only be a registered voter to call one of these shows and complain about the way things are? What if you had to actually participate in democracy rather than sit on your can all day? Would there be any change in the whining level whatsoever? Who knows, maybe there would. I know the late Walter Matthau would have taken the bet there would have been a different tone in the callers. Of course, knowing Walter as I did, he'd have taken the bet going the other way too if it was offered and he could have set the odds.

Most of America listens to the radio in the car. I was in that group. So as I drove, it became a routine to answer questions or make comments. Usually it was coming home from lunch, and on the day of the Paula Jones ruling, I was going down K Street trying to make the turn on 19th Street and saying to Rush for all to hear, "If he did it, he'll face the music so calm down." One day, as I was yelling at the radio, some guy with an Orioles cap standing at 19th and K yelled, "That's right, Larry. Give 'em hell!" I thought he agreed with the cogent points I was making until the next day I made the same turn at the same time and hadn't said a word to Rush and the guy is standing in the same place and starts waving and yelling, "That's right, Larry. Give 'em hell." And to think there could have been a groundswell building.

The issue was the topic at lunch, however. I was alone at Jack Kent Cooke's table but that didn't stop my mind from covering all the bases. I think I had Bill Clinton figured out. He is the uncle that is in every family. He is smart and loud and drives the neatest car and obviously is doing something right. But everybody talks about him when he isn't in the room. "You know what I heard?" they would say and then, in hushed tones, say it. He is the one who will come up to you when you're a kid and when nobody is around and ask, "How are the girls?" And then he would look around to make sure nobody is watching and hand you ten dollars saying "Don't tell anyone" while pinching your cheek. And you know what? You don't tell anyone because you like him. The ten spot has nothing to do with it. I had this figured out before the tuna salad arrived.

Two months earlier, Washington attorney Bob Bennett had been hired by the White House to handle the case of Paula Jones versus Bill Clinton. He was the brother of Bill Bennett, education secretary under Ronald Reagan, drug czar, and best-selling author (*The Book of Virtues*). I wondered that year what Christmas dinner would be like at the Bennett house with one brother representing the president of the United States against charges that he had tried, as governor, to get sexual favors from a state employee, and the other being the expert on virtuous behavior and goals. On the night of the ruling, Bennett sat with me in the Washington studio. I told him before we went on I was looking forward to a segment that had nothing to do with O.J. And of course you know what the first question was? It wasn't planned but after a while we become conditioned, I guess. See, talk about something long enough and it becomes part of the DNA. Bennett played it as the good lawyer he is: no comment. But he did talk about the other topic, which hadn't come up at lunch anywhere for a long time, a topic that was headed for hearings in the House and Senate: Whitewater.

> BENNETT: I certainly think that this investigation is what's being done now, it's an appropriate thing to do. I candidly think that these congressional investigations are a waste of time and a waste of taxpayer money. Certainly, I don't know how you really justify in a commonsense view the House doing it and then the Senate doing it, then Fiske doing it and, I think the whole Whitewater thing is much ado about nothing. And it's just a reflection of our time, where we try to criminalize everything.
> KING: This is one tough town, is it not?
> BENNETT: New York is a tough town, Larry. This is a mean town.

The "meanness" in town, whether it really exists or is part of the White House spin that anyone who disagrees is a Hater, combined with a need to become politically effective again, pushed the White House to make a change in job assignments, moving Mack McLarty out of the chief of staff position and replacing him with Leon Panetta, a former director of the Office of Management and Budget, chairman of the House Budget Committee, and a California congressman whose district included Monterey. The Clinton White House was having a hell of a time getting legislation through Congress and the feeling was, maybe one of their own would open some doors that had been closed. As a matter of fact I had both McLarty and Panetta on the night the change was announced, but only for a half hour. The second half of the show was about, well, you know what it was about.

But I hadn't forgotten Clinton's promise to show up for an hour (or was it an hour and a half?) every six months. The staff called the White House months in advance to get the interview on the schedule and when nothing seemed to be working they asked me to just pick up the phone and call the president of the United States. I could imagine the scene:

> Mr. President? You have the Prime Minister of
> Pakistan in the Roosevelt Room and he says he has
> the nuclear capability to bomb the hell out of India if
> they tick him off. You also have a conference call
> with the OAS chairman on aid to Haiti. Newt
> Gingrich is here for a meeting you wanted set up to
> talk about common ground. Oh, and Larry King is on
> the phone. Which would you like to do first?

The interview didn't happen. And I had to wonder, if we could have O.J. in the studio to put his side of the story out there or Bill Clinton to talk about the bad time he's been having and both were only available on the same day, who would be the guest that night? No question, I would ask the president if we could reschedule for another time.

The news of the summer was (1) the O.J. trial had a tentative mid-September start date that everyone knew wasn't going to happen and (2) the idiots running baseball were going to let a strike take place. The baseball story was simpler. Money was driving both the players and the owners. This wasn't a newsflash because both sides were saying to anyone who would listen, it *was* an issue about money. The owners wanted to cap the salaries and use the savings for franchises (like Pittsburgh and Milwaukee) in financial need. The players said if they are worth $1,875,358.75 a year, then they ought to be paid that amount. It reminded me of a conversation I'd had with Jackie Gleason back in the 1960s when he did his television show from Miami.

"Nobody is overpaid," he said.

"Nobody?"

"Look, if there's someone willing to pay whatever the amount is, then how can you say the person getting that salary is overpaid?" I couldn't argue with the logic. Still can't.

As was the case with any baseball fan, I missed the game. And I understood the positions taken by both sides. Labor Secretary Robert Reich told me it was going to be tough for either side to garner support from the fan level because the average player salary was a million dollars a year. But the issue was (that word again) moot. For instance, Barry Bonds makes $8 million a year with the San Francisco Giants while somewhere in America a cop makes $41,500. Everyone will agree a cop is more important to society than a baseball player. But is Bonds gonna say "sorry, can't take the $8 million because a cop is worth more than I am"? Jackie Gleason died in 1987 but he sure knew a lot about 1994. By the way, the baseball strike forced the cancellation of the World Series because it lasted 234 days. It was a diversion, if only for a few seconds, from what was being called the Trial of the Century.

As this was going on, my senior executive producer, Wendy Walker Whitworth, had put together a wonderful trio of experts to explain what the hell had happened that day in the O.J. case, since we were all covering it and a lot of people, including Larry King, didn't understand all the talk about the Griffin Rule or exculpatory evidence that was going on live across TV screens every day. We had a judge from L.A. Superior Court, Jack Tenner, who had retired and was known for his handling of Michael Jackson's trial when the singer was sued for allegedly taking sexual advantage of a boy (Jackson later settled out of court). We had the former attorney general under Ronald Reagan, Dick Thornburgh, who had also been Pennsylvania's governor and a prosecutor, and we had defense attorney Gerry Spence, who had yet to lose a jury trial. It was a great combination of résumés and attitudes. And throughout the 153 years the O.J. trial went on, we brought them back as often as possible to help explain the day. And on the second show we did, talk turned to betting.

Here was the situation: We covered how much of a blood sample was needed for DNA since prosecutor Marcia Clark had made it clear she would have blood taken from O.J.'s Bronco matched with blood at the crime scene. And I knew we were going to have to get into a commercial break within a minute, so I asked what I thought to be a simple sum-it-up question.

> KING: Just from what you know, on a scale of
> 1 to 10, the prosecution is at about a what
> to you?
> THORNBURGH: It's about a 5 and rising, I'd
> say.
> KING: 5? Not an 8 or a 9?
> THORNBURGH: No, I think there are many
> uncertainties. Obviously, the results of the
> DNA tests are going to be crucial . . . until
> you have that, you can't push them over
> the top with a 10.
> KING: Let me get a break. We'll be back with
> Spence, Tenner, and Thornburgh on *Larry
> King Live*.
> TENNER: I would say at the moment the
> prosecution is about a 6½ favorite.
> SPENCE: Well I agree with Mr. Thornburgh.

I had a producer screaming in my earpiece to get into the commercial and I put up my hand as a traffic cop would to get the trio to just shut up for a minute (actually two minutes). But it went on through the commercial as well. By the time we came back on, everyone had an opinion and was pumped to let it be known. I reintroduced the guests and then looked to Gerry Spence in his trademark suede jacket.

> KING: The judge rates it 6½ point favorite.
> Dick Thornburgh says 5 and rising on a
> scale of 10. Your call now, and then we'll go
> back to calls—

SPENCE: You are something else. Because what
    you're doing is asking us to try this case
    based on what we've heard in the press.
KING: From what we know to this point.
SPENCE: Yeah, so what I—
KING: —That's what everybody's doing at the
    bars and restaurants.
SPENCE: Yeah, so, isn't that something, that
    we're trying the O.J. Simpson case based on
    the press? And we're—
KING: —Such is life.
SPENCE: Yeah, so it is, life.

I understood Gerry's concern. Certainly, you could play this on the high ground and not discuss the matter until there was a verdict, which is what is done in England. But you know what? It drew the audience in. The backyard fence now included the voices of Spence-Tenner-and-Thornburgh (one of the jokes during commercials was the fact this could become a do-it-yourself legal team for hire with a traveling defense attorney, prosecuting attorney, and judge). High road or not, this was healthy.

With five weeks before the November election, the producers at *Larry King Live* were able to get the two candidates for the Senate from California to be in the same room and speak out on issues national as well as local. It was the first time the two had debated each other. Dianne Feinstein was completing her first term in the Senate and faced a major challenge from Michael Huffington, a wealthy Republican oilman. In fact, the race was drawing national attention not only because Huffington had closed a thirty-point deficit to single digits, but because it was the most expensive Senate campaign to date. By the time they sat together in the Washington studio, each had spent close to $10 million for a job that paid a little over $100,000. And it was not only an expensive campaign but it was nasty.

These two people did not like each other. The Feinstein camp was telling everyone it would be the first opportunity to take the race beyond paid advertising, and the Huffington-backers were saying anytime the voters get to ask their incumbent senator a question, that's a victory. The ground rules were that once we took the air, no aide or advisor would be allowed to talk to their boss until after the entire show was done. "What you see is what you get" is the way I explained our rules.

Feinstein didn't talk to Huffington and he didn't talk to her until the show began. Then I couldn't keep them from taking shots at each other. By the time we got to a commercial I decided to try and settle them both down, so I talked about how well each was doing and how we're all going to have some fun and learn about the issues, and isn't it wonderful the public has the opportunity to participate? Huffington and Feinstein said nothing. They didn't even look at each other. The room temperature was dropping. To this day when I'm asked what was the toughest show to do, the Huffington-Feinstein debate is right up there. But it was great television and it was the night I started thinking how this could be a way to teach students in high school debate class what to do and what not to do, it could be a way for a civics class to discuss how two people see the same world differently, and it could be a great political science or journalism class on what television is doing to, or for, the political scene.

Twenty-four hours later I was standing on the balcony of

a home overlooking the San Fernando Valley, in the state that would soon have a senator named Huffington or Feinstein. And I was thinking about the song "What a Diff'rence a Day Makes" by Diana Washington because standing next to me was Marlon Brando. A week earlier my office had called me in Los Angeles to say Brando had finally agreed to an interview but wanted to talk with me first. And within five minutes of getting that phone call, the phone rang again.

"Larry, this is Marlon."

"Marlon who?" I asked.

There was a pause. "Marlon Brando."

"Hey, it could have been Marlin Fitzwater," I said and he started laughing.

"I want to talk before we do this so let's have lunch here," he said and I explained I didn't have a car. Marlon told me he would send a driver to bring me over and gave me his address. So I went downstairs at the Beverly Wilshire and waited for my ride. After a few moments a white Chevy pulls up. I'm standing there waiting for a limo or a Lincoln when, for whatever reason, I look into the Chevy. Brando is behind the wheel. He motions for me to get in and the hotel doorman is standing there saying, "I'm seeing this and I don't believe this." He wasn't the only one feeling that way.

Somehow we both started trying to top each other with song lyrics. He started the words to a Sinatra song and I would finish and then I'd do the same and he would finish the words. We went through the Gershwin list. And then I started asking him about acting and he brushed all my questions aside. Brando pulled over, stopped the car, and said to me slowly, "All of us are actors." He picked up an imaginary phone and says, "Larry, this is Marlon. Your father is dead." I'm sitting there looking at him and I say something like gee that's too bad and I can't believe it and I start picking up the situation and we go back and forth in the imaginary conversation. I forgot, for a moment, that I'm sitting in a car at an expired parking meter with Marlon Brando making up a conversation with an imaginary phone in my hand. After we hung up our phones he looked at me and said I did well and made the point that what we had just done in a car on a Beverly Hills street was no different from what actors do every day. He started driving again and we did "I've Got a Date with an Angel" making the turn off Rodeo Drive.

The conversations in the car and at lunch turned up in the interview. We were set up at his house and as I started asking questions about acting I realized Marlon was barefoot. What the hell, I thought, he's at home. His dog even came on camera for a while.

> KING: Why did you choose acting as a career? Why did you choose to be other people?
>
> BRANDO: I think it's useful to make an observation that everybody here in this room is an actor; you're an actor. And the best performance that I've ever seen is when the director says "cut" and the director says, "That was great. That was wonderful. That was good, except here were a few, we had a little lighting problem. Let's do it again." What he's thinking is "Jesus Christ, that's so fucking—excuse me—it's that it wasn't done well so we've got to do it over."

For whatever reason, I didn't flinch when he used the F word although the control room people were right on the button to bleep it out. But I was getting used to "Mr. B." as I called him and his language wasn't unexpected. And the only reason I can offer is because with Brando, everything is unexpected. Anything he does is himself.

Toward the end of the interview the songs began. He suggested "Limehouse Blues" from *Ziegfield Follies*, but I didn't know the words. So we went back to another Gershwin tune, "I Can't Get Started with You." As we finished the first stanza I said good night to the audience and the next thing I knew, Brando leaned over and kissed me right on the lips. I was stunned. And I just knew what was being said in the control room thousands of miles away. I've never done that with a man on the first date but I will tell you, even now, I think about him and that's without a Gershwin tune driving the moment.

When we were done Brando got up and started handing out glasses to the crew and then poured champagne for everyone. It was after our ninety minutes that I realized there is no indication this is the house of an actor. He didn't know where his Oscar was and didn't care. The paintings and photos on the wall have nothing to do with film or the stage. In fact, the only place I saw a profession-related photo was in his bathroom where there was a black-and-white from *A Streetcar Named Desire*. The time with Brando was wonderful and I asked him to consider another session (for an interview not the other thing). He readily agreed. It was a terrific break from O.J. and midterm elections. And it was good to meet a guy who knew more Gershwin than I did. We should always work with someone better. That's how we grow.

With less than a week before the November election, the White House called to say the president had room in his schedule for an interview on Sunday while he was in Seattle. He was five months late on the every-six-months promise but we, of course, agreed. Whenever the White House tells you there is "room on the schedule," the real meaning is we need to get The Message Out. The stupid polls asking voters "if the election were held today, blah blah blah" were all showing that a bad time was in store for Democrats in the twelve governorships, thirty-six Senate seats, and all of the House. I had been consistent in my dismissal of the "if-question" polls until now. It wasn't because of any deep feeling I had from talking with people in my travels or even from phone calls on the television show. It was because polls were even looking bad for Mario Cuomo in his bid to be New York governor for a fourth straight term. In my simplistic view of the world via Brooklyn, it seemed if Cuomo wasn't gonna make it, then all other Democrats were in trouble. It was to be one of the few accurate political observations of my career.

I met Clinton at the Assisted Living of America headquarters on a brilliant Seattle afternoon where he had been meeting with senior citizens and talking about health care. He campaigned that day for a member of the King County Council who was trying to unseat Republican Slade Gorton in the Senate. We spoke briefly about how he saw events on election day, now forty-eight hours away, and Clinton said it was going to be tough. He knew. I knew he knew there was going to be a Republican shakeup in Congress. But he still had the smile and the optimism and that's what he expressed on the air. As he spoke about the importance of "not being able to afford to give in to the blamers instead of the builders," I thought to myself, "Why doesn't he just stop in mid-sentence and say, 'Larry, we're gonna get killed at the polls on Tuesday.'"

Midterm elections are always tough for the party that is trying to get in. If we elect a president of one party, then there seems to be a need to elect a Congress of the other party. I can only guess it's because on that one day in third grade when the teacher talked about the system of checks and balances, everyone was paying attention.

But what I took away from that hour with Bill Clinton was how he had changed. He had been beaten up, he had become smarter about the way things work in Washington, and, maybe more important, how things don't work in Washington. The man who had campaigned on the theme of change had, himself, changed.

Speaking of which, there had been rumors circulating that personnel changes were about to happen at the White House and so I tried to get him to comment. I asked about Secretary of State Warren Christopher staying on the job but Clinton wasn't letting on at all. Press Secretary Dee Dee Myers was sitting just a few feet away and her name had been among those rumored to be on the way out as well. It's tough to know the person and also have them nearby while asking their boss if he was keeping them on the job.

> KING: Do you want her to stay?
> CLINTON: She's doing a good job. And she's
> going to stay as long as we decide she's
> going to stay, she and I together.
> KING: First time the whole night you've been
> a little—
> CLINTON: Oh, I've been a little evasive on all
> personnel questions.

KING: You don't want to discuss personnel?
CLINTON: I think presidents should always be
slightly evasive on personnel questions
unless there is some great policy issue
involved.

I could tell Dee Dee was hurt by the answer. I was surprised by it. And I wasn't buying any of this and Bill Clinton knew it. You reach a point where you either hammer the guy who doesn't want to answer the question by asking the same thing in as many different ways as possible or you just say the hell with it and move on to the next topic. I chose the latter. But I knew there was something going on.

After the interview I went back to my hotel, where, of course, I picked up the clicker and started going through the channels trying to find ESPN. And that made me think of a question I had been meaning to ask Bill Clinton: Why can't ESPN have the same channel regardless of the city? As I was going through the 159 different stations the phone rang. I picked it up on the first ring.

"Larry? Bill Clinton." I knew the voice. He was calling from his limo heading toward the airport. "Larry, I've really been thinking about that part of the interview where I talked about Dee Dee. You gotta help me here, pal. I need you to cut that part out."

"Mr. President, it's not my call but I'll get ahold of Tom Johnson (CNN president) right away and get an answer for you," I said, all the time knowing the request didn't have a snowball's chance in hell. He thanked me and as I put the receiver back on the phone I remembered the most important question of the day. I was too late. He had hung up. For just a moment, I thought about just staying on the line and waiting for him to pick up the phone again but I wasn't sure if phones still worked that way and, besides, I had found ESPN anyway. I called Tom Johnson and was told there was no way we were going to edit the interview. CNN called the White House back to give them the news. Dee Dee Myers resigned as White House spokesperson the following month.

On November 8, Democratic governors in eleven states were removed, every Republican in the Senate and House was reelected, and for the first time in forty years, Democrats didn't control the lower house of Congress. Mario Cuomo lost to George Pataki in New York. It was, to say the least, a rout.

A little more than a month before this stampede, Republicans had gathered on the steps of the Capitol to announce, if elected or reelected, they were going to push a Contract With America through the 104th Congress within its first hundred days. And as I watched this taking place on television, which is how most of the country learned about the plan, I figured I had missed the boat somewhere. For one, I didn't recall signing any contract or, for that matter, agreeing to any contract. And if I had, it sure wouldn't include a constitutional amendment to balance the budget because that could be done anytime by the current members of the House and Senate. We've spent more time arguing about the need, or against the need, for that amendment than we have in actually balancing the budget.

The Contract called for term limits, which, while well intentioned, implies voters aren't smart enough to make the right decision more than once or twice or whatever the term limit becomes. And it throws the good legislators out. I thought those two elements of the Contract were ridiculous and designed for lazy voters and undisciplined members of Congress. It was making democracy easy and it was governing by remote control instead of getting up off your ass and changing the channel yourself if that's what you wanted done. We did a number of interviews with proponents and opponents of the Contract and, as always, I kept my views to myself. The show has never been about what I think and feel; it's about how the major players in an issue think and feel. That's why it works.

The Trial of the Century began with wall-to-wall coverage by CNN, CNBC, E!, and Court TV to name just a few. In addition, the networks interrupted soap operas and local affiliates knocked off the syndicated talk shows with weeping victims in order to provide viewers with a dose of O.J. Ratings soared and the O.J. story became a part of our culture, and I'm not sure if it still isn't that way. When all of this started back in June of 1994, CNN had won fourteen of the top fifteen Nielsen-rated cable slots (and we would have had a sweep had it not been for the Stanley Cup playoffs. I was mortified to be beaten by a hockey game; especially after listening to Bob Costas tell me hockey would never make it on television). Marcia Clark and Christopher Darden and Lance Ito and Robert Shapiro, F. Lee Bailey, Johnnie Cochran, and even the court reporter all became a part of our homes. Herb Cohen was right. It was a miniseries. We knew the names and the personalities. We all admired Cochran's ties and Marcia Clark's hair and we all had discussions about what was with all the hourglasses around Judge Ito and what was on his laptop computer screen (the theory at lunch in both Washington and Los Angeles was he had a hell of a solitaire game going). Prior to the start of the trial, CNN and other news organizations had been asked by Judge Ito to avoid running interviews with Faye Resnick, who knew Nicole Brown Simpson and O.J. and had written a Get-It-On-The-Shelves-Fast book about her experiences with them both. Ito was concerned about pretrial publicity, since a jury had yet to be seated and I was keenly aware this, and future trials, were going to have to deal with the newfound speed in our culture. Bill Clinton in Seattle had told me the trial shouldn't even be on television until a jury was selected. CNN agreed to Ito's request.

The day the decision was announced to hold off on interviewing Resnick, Judge Ito faxed me a thank-you letter that, somehow, ended up in the *New York Times*. You ever have your home phone number published in the *New York Times*? I had the number changed the next day to fend off all the wacko disc jockeys trying to either be profound or funny or, as was the case, neither. Ito invited me to visit his chambers and that was an offer I wasn't going to let pass. We set a day and I showed up as scheduled taking the elevator to his chambers during the lunch recess.

I knew a few guys named Lance in Brooklyn and, suffice it to say, they were not guys I made a point to run with very often if ever. But Judge Ito couldn't have been nicer and we spent almost an hour talking about how his life has changed and what he wants to do after O.J. and about the mail he gets and, of course, television in the courtroom. After a while I told him I'd better go because I didn't want to delay the trial and stood up. Judge Ito smiled and said, "Larry, I am the trial. I decide when it starts." With that, he got up and shook my hand. I told him he should do the show when all of this is over. Ito looked at me. His face said "don't ask that question again."

115

I left the cubbyhole chambers and walked down the hall thinking this is how I came in. It wasn't. It was Judge Ito's courtroom and the next thing I knew I'm standing there looking at O.J. and Shapiro and Marcia Clark and trying to figure how Larry is gonna get out of this one.

"Hey Larry!" O.J. said.

"Juice, good to see you," I said. Shapiro was there and I nodded and then I figured I better acknowledge the prosecution as well, so I went over and said hello to them.

Walking out of the building all I could feel was relief that I'd finally found daylight. That's when I looked up to see 187 reporters standing in front of me.

"Hey Larry, what's going on?"

"Hey Larry, did O.J. talk to you?"

"Larry, is it true you are a character witness for O.J.?"

I looked at them all and said "no comment" eleven times and walked away. All the time I was thinking to myself, "Man I hope it's over," adding "now."

Larry King Live producers had been talking with Robert Shapiro's office all along letting him know that of all the venues available when he decided to talk, this television show was the one to do. When I was in Washington, Shapiro had called me saying let's have dinner and he gave me his cell phone number with instructions to let him know when I'm heading to Los Angeles and he'll get me on his schedule. Well, we made plans to do a week in L.A. and my first thought was to get ahold of Shapiro and set up a dinner. I was sitting in my condo with the O.J. trial on TV as I dialed the number and I had made a list of places I was going to suggest for dinner. I had always liked the dining room in the Four Seasons on Doheny and the staff was always very good about setting up a private table, which, considering the horde of reporters probably following his every move, would make Shapiro feel as comfortable as possible. So I had pretty much decided my first suggestion would be the Four Seasons as I watched TV while listening to the phone ring.

And on TV a phone started ringing in the courtroom. Ito interrupted the proceedings and started yelling about who had the cell phone, and all the time I'm sitting there on my white sofa with a phone in my hand sipping coffee with a list of possible dinner places on the table not realizing what is actually happening. Sometimes, 1 plus 1 doesn't equal 2.

I watched Shapiro stand up and open a briefcase and then look to Judge Ito. "Your honor, my sincerest apologies. I simply forgot to turn off my phone. It won't happen again."

The judge started saying something to Shapiro and that's when I realized the ringing had stopped on the number I had just dialed. And so I figured we had just been disconnected and I started dialing the number Shapiro had given me again when suddenly I understood what had just occurred. Let me put it this way, I had a real bad feeling. And when I looked back at the television, Ito was still talking to Shapiro. Technology can be a wonderful thing, if you can add.

When I got to CNN that night we had booked a return visit of what had come to be known as "the trio": Judge Tenner, defense attorney Gerry Spence, and former attorney general Dick Thornburgh. There was one moment when I thought, since nothing is inside anymore, since we talk about every nuance occurring in the courtroom, I ought to ask them how some idiot could call Robert Shapiro on a cell phone and not realize Shapiro was in the middle of the most important case of his career? I didn't. Some things ought to be just left alone. After all, we were being accused every single moment of overcoverage. And even if these were times when anything goes, that doesn't mean you gotta always go along with it.

CHAPTER FIVE

Seeing Is Believing

February 1995. It has been a few years since CNN permanently put its logo on the bottom right-hand corner of the television screen. My first impression was why keep telling me I'm watching CNN when I already know I'm watching CNN? And is the logo blocking anything I should be seeing? After three minutes, I got used to it.

As is the case in television, which constantly makes noise about being such a creative medium, the logo started appearing on every other network a few minutes after CNN put it there. Fox used it during football games. The logo was in front of the viewer to subtly tell them this is what you have on or, if used somewhere else, this is what you missed by not having it on. In fact, take a look at the screen right now and you'll see logo evolution with not just the network symbol but the time, the temperature, the latest NASDAQ, lotto numbers, and what you owe Visa.

I brought this well-thought-out observation to lunch at The Palm one day and sat by myself. Herb Cohen was just leaving after a working lunch with clients. He sat down at my table and made the mistake of asking "what's new?" and in I started about the TV logo in the corner and how it's a new way of keeping the name in front of the viewer. Herbie listened for all of one minute before putting up his hand, stopping me in mid-sentence.

"Larry, you know who that is over there?" he said, pointing to a table full of guys having what appeared to be a serious conversation. I recognized one of them.

"Yeah, that's Ben Bradlee. He's on all the time with me."

"You ever read the newspaper Ben works for?"

"Every morning. It's delivered to my door. The *Washington Post*." I had no idea where this was going.

"Okay, at the top of every page in the newspaper that you read today what did it say?"

"It says the *Washington Post* and it tells me the date."

"And you're gonna tell me—"

"The logo—"

"This is something new because TV does it?"

He had me.

"Larry, I gotta go." And Herb was gone. And all I could think about was what had happened to my logo theory. I looked at some of the others in the restaurant that day having lunch. Over to my right (don't start the symbolism thing) was Dan Quayle's former chief of staff, Bill Kristol, who was a regular when a Sunday talk show needed a conservative pundit. And straight ahead, Bob Beckel was having lunch with someone whose back was to me. Beckel had run Walter Mondale's 1984 presidential campaign against Ronald Reagan and, well, let's say Beckel was now making a good living as a pundit on the left and leave it at that. Both were talented guys (Beckel came up with the "where's the beef?" line for Mondale during a debate with Gary Hart) who were plugged into their party's message and agenda and, maybe most important of all, could present the views with plain talk. For just a moment I thought about the television screen and pictured both Beckel and Kristol on *Larry King Live* with a graphic identifying who each was, their background, and then their percentage of accuracy in making predictions about particular issues. They could be debating, for instance, Clinton's foreign aid budget and we'd see a graphic next to each giving the number of times they have been right about a congressional subcommittee approving Administration spending plans.

Look at it this way, no pun intended, baseball and football do it all the time. You get Sammy Sosa's number of times at bat, his percentage against a particular team, his percentage getting home runs in the bottom of the seventh as compared to any other time, the number of bases he can get to if he fails to hit it out of the park, the number of times he gets a hit when Clinton is out of the country, and all the other statistics one needs to enjoy the game. My concern was one can know too much and not be able to understand what's taking place on the screen or the field with all the statistics getting in the way. The scary thought was, someday a *Larry King Live* viewer could see such a graphic on their screen displaying the number of times Larry has used the phrase "we have a lot of bases to cover" or the number of times he has talked to Mel Brooks or the last date he wore that particular pair of braces. The comforting thought was my prediction statistics probably would remain consistent.

All of this hit me while watching O.J. because, since he

had taken over afternoons on the East Coast, stations were using split screens and news crawls to let the viewer know the world hadn't stopped and that other issues, like the temperature, were still occurring on a regular basis. The times made O.J. an industry. Court TV and CNBC and, of course, CNN had attorneys ready to go on camera whenever there was a break in the trial. CNN hired trial lawyer Greta Van Susteren and former prosecutor Roger Cossack on a per diem basis to explain what the viewers had just seen and help everyone understand where each side was trying to go. There was no difference between having Greta and Roger on camera to describe the events in the courtroom and that of O.J. on camera telling Bob Costas what had just happened on the football field.

Long before there was talk of a Trial of the Century, there was a 1996 campaign for president of the United States. Before O.J. even went to trial, there were White House meetings to set in place a run for the second term. And there were numerous meetings outside the White House to discuss a run against the guy who was going to go for a second term. Bob Dole was one such person and, with his Washington experience, had the nomination to lose. And from the get-go, it was clear the people around Bob Dole had learned from the events of four years earlier. After the CNN show one night I picked up the remote control and saw David Letterman interviewing Dole. He didn't say he was a candidate but he said he was going to run.

Two thoughts smacked me in the head: (1) Isn't it insane we can mince words in such a way so that we can say we are going to do something, but yet that still doesn't put us in the category of someone who is going to do something?

Now, I'm aware Dole can't say he's a candidate because then he falls under the equal time rule for broadcast networks and anything he says will be viewed by editors as a campaign issue rather than as something important to his job as Senate majority leader. Still, you could have just landed from Pluto and not be able to speak English and still know Dole is a candidate and is going to run. It's a stupid game played by all of us and it makes me put the clicker to work whenever I watch the C-SPAN academics wringing their hands as to reasons there are disenfranchised Americans who don't go to the polls (and that's where I had been before going to Letterman. My evening is worldly: ESPN, C-SPAN, CNN, Letterman, and then repeat the routine ten times in an hour). (2) Bob Dole was playing to the Letterman audience to let them know he could be their president and he was willing to come to them rather than expect them to go to him. And it was a variation on a theme played by both Bill Clinton and Ross Perot— going outside of what had once been the usual way of getting a message to people who might pay attention. If nothing else, Bob Dole had learned from George Bush.

With the New Hampshire primary just a year away, producers at *Larry King Live* started having conversations with candidates ready to be the next president. Though he couldn't say he was running, Dole came on to talk about why he wanted to run. He was going to be seventy-three and refused to state he would only serve one term if elected. I thought that made a lot of sense. What if he had a great presidency? What if the country surged ahead? Would he then say "sorry, but I made a promise"? And what would that do to others who are the same age? It was a nonissue. But this was a time when nonissues abounded. Still, Dole was a candidate, even though he couldn't say he was a candidate. And that got me going:

125

KING: You go on Letterman and you
   announce. You crushed us.
DOLE: No, that was an informal
   announcement.
KING: Because you can informally announce
   here again, right?
DOLE: Well, we're going to really announce on
   April 10.
KING: How are you going to do it? Where are
   you going to be?
DOLE: We're going to start in Topeka and then
   go to Des Moines and then Concord, New
   Hampshire; end up that night in New York
   City, and then we're going to be around for
   a while. Then I end up in my hometown of
   Russell, Kansas.
KING: And then here again?
DOLE: And then back here.

He wasn't gonna do a Perot and I never expected him
to do it. Dole had an organized campaign in the works and
to say what everyone knew he was going to say before April
10 didn't make any sense. But, indeed, Indiana senator
Richard Lugar came on to say he was in, Dan Quayle came
on to say he wasn't. Pat Buchanan and California congressman Robert Dornan both came on within a day of each other
saying they were candidates. It was a routine I enjoyed. And,
more important, having these intelligent people in a studio
answering questions from viewers was as good for the voter
as it was for the candidate. And maybe it was good for the
nonvoter as well? It made me wonder why we hadn't been
doing it all along.

It being a new campaign, I had to ask Bob Dole the Veep Question. My opinion hadn't changed one iota as to the chances he would answer it, but one just never knows. In fact, after asking the question to everyone during campaigns since 6 B.C., my feeling that I would get an answer about a vice president from Dole when he wouldn't even officially say he was a candidate was slimmer than ever. There is something to be said for a gut feeling:

> KING: Are you going to name a vice president early?
>
> DOLE: I don't think so.
>
> KING: I thought you were going to.
>
> DOLE: Well, I think it's an option just like the one-term thing, you know. It may happen but I think it's too early to tell.
>
> KING: Rumors that Colin Powell has told friends that he'd like to run with you. Would that be a given? If Colin Powell called tomorrow and said, "I'd like to be your running mate," would you announce that tomorrow?
>
> DOLE: Well, I don't think that will happen. I'm not trying to duck the question and I don't think he said that.
>
> KING: It's a hypothetical.
>
> DOLE: I know it's a hypothetical but you know, Pete Wilson [governor of delegate-rich California] might call. I might have two on the line at the same time, or maybe Carroll Campbell [former South Carolina governor].

> KING: Can we say Colin would be high on the
>   list?
> DOLE: He'd be very high on a very fairly short
>   list.

I decided after that interview with Bob Dole that I would continue to ask the Veep Question because (1) anyone thinking about running for the job has got to be thinking about who might have to take over should something go wrong and because (2), very simply, how can you not ask it?

Just before the Contract With America was going to hit the Hundred Day Mark, Newt Gingrich came on to talk about life as speaker of the House. The Contract had eight of the ten elements approved by House Republicans and it was pretty clear they were going to lose on the term limits issue. I asked him other things; like how the end of the Cold War, and the fact there was no enemy, made it difficult for Republicans to define themselves? Newt said it wasn't just Republicans with that problem.

> KING: There is no world villain though, is
>   there?
> GINGRICH: No.
> KING: I mean there is the Husseins—
> GINGRICH: No. We're in a different world.
> KING: There's no Stalin.
> GINGRICH: No. We're in a world that's a
>   mess, but it's not a menace, if I can make
>   that distinction.
> KING: So what change is that bringing us? We
>   don't have a universal person to hate.

GINGRICH: Yeah, I'll tell you what we've got
to think through, and this is a real
challenge to us as a people. I believe we
have a duty to lead because nobody else
can.

We went to a commercial break and Newt leaned over
to talk about coverage. He made the point the press never
mentioned Roosevelt was in a wheelchair, adding that as a
result many in the country never knew. He was right. And
he was right about another point he made during the commercial: that wouldn't be happening today. We know more
and there's not a darn thing anyone can do about it.

The upcoming election, and in 1995 "upcoming" meant
nineteen months away, interfered with President Clinton's
attempt to have a prime-time news conference about welfare
reform in April. He'd only had four of them since getting to
the White House and I had been making the point that this
in itself was news, so it ought to be carried. CNN, of course,
carried it, as did CBS, but NBC chose to stay with *Frasier*
and ABC went with *Home Improvement.* This wasn't the first
time a president had been turned down on news conference
coverage. George Bush announced he would answer questions
in June 1992 and nobody carried it, citing this was a campaign event rather than a matter requiring public awareness
of a presidential decision or issue. I could understand the networks wanting to keep the revenue for ads on prime-time
shows rather than losing it to coverage of questionable
news. The issue, then, was whether the Clinton White
House had properly explained the newsworthiness in the
president's appearance before reporters. The answer was
nope. There wasn't any news to offer. At least the O.J. trial,

which sometimes actually had news, provided opportunities for commercial breaks when Judge Ito called a court recess.

But there was a larger issue going on that day and it continues to this moment. And it came to my attention in a conversation I had with presidential historian Doris Kearns Goodwin. In these days of five hundred channels on television and five hundred special interest magazines for specific segments of the public and the fact that newspapers, by their nature, can't reach the public until the day after an event, a president is going to have one hell of a time trying to capture the attention of America. Because the audience is so fragmented, a presidential news conference reaches only a specific group while missing many others. Roosevelt used to have a fireside chat and everyone tuned in to hear his words. A big problem for the White House too was keeping the president from being overexposed. That's why the news conferences were infrequent. Wacko as it seems, in the multi-channel universe it's tougher for Bill Clinton to reach a broad swath of America now than it was for Roosevelt with only radio.

I'd had the same discussion with media critic Howard Kurtz of the *Washington Post* and asked him if we might someday look back at these times and say it was a transition period. His answer was yes. "We have clearly left the old black-and-white days behind when there were three networks and everyone watched Ed Sullivan," he said, "but I don't think we've quite arrived at the brave new world of the future." In a way, it was comforting to know we are still learning how to do this and, similarly, the White House was probably learning as well. And yet, in another way, it was frustrating because I knew there was a way for a president to be able to reach the national community if an issue required him or her to do so. But I hadn't a clue as to where the way was to be found.

The way was found on April 19 at 9:02 A.M. Central Time in Oklahoma City when the nine-story Alfred P. Murrah Federal Building was leveled by a bomb. Within hours, everyone knew what had happened, and as the day went on, more and more people tuned in CNN or each of the networks as newsrooms launched into a familiar routine: nonstop coverage. Twelve hours after it happened I was talking to Oklahoma governor Frank Keating, who stood in front of the disaster scene. As I spoke to him, it became clear the public's attention can be found if the voice seeking it is loud enough. Oklahoma City was such a voice:

> You know, we come together as one people when
> things like this happen. President Clinton is of an
> opposite political party than I but he is very sincere
> and outraged and angry about what occurred here,
> because this was an attack on defenseless people, on
> children. I just can't imagine something like this
> happening in a civilized society.

Had you told me earlier that I'd be talking to the governor of Oklahoma in the first segment of the show that evening I'd have asked what Keating had to do with O.J. Simpson. Twenty-four hours later, Attorney General Janet Reno announced that a $2 million reward was being offered for information leading to the arrest of those responsible. Suddenly, the show was being used as a version of *America's Most Wanted* and it was happening because everyone was paying attention. I asked former FBI and CIA director William Webster about it on the second evening:

You want the immediate attention of the American people before these people can disappear in the woodwork. They may have a different name. They may be recognized under a different set of facts that could be plugged into the computers and more quickly identify who they are and where they're apt to be located.

Within a week of the bombing, one suspect, Timothy McVeigh, was arrested. Investigators were still looking for "John Doe No. 2" and the television show put a police sketch of him on to assist in the search. In a way, we were the post office bulletin board as well as the back fence. Both had been around for years, which was proof, again, that everything I was doing every night on television really was nothing new. We were taking the human need to be connected and using technology. Same game, just different toys.

President Clinton and Vice President Gore made an appearance on a special Sunday night edition of *Larry King Live* (by this time we were way off the every-six-months routine) and it was the first time the two most powerful people in the country had ever appeared together for a live interview program.

We were now seventeen months away from the 1996 election, so one of the first questions was similar to my earlier interview with Bob Dole, and with a similar answer.

> KING: And are you two definitely running
> again as a ticket?
> GORE: We're not ready to make any
> announcement.

KING: Oh come on, make it. Everyone makes
  it here.
CLINTON: I haven't asked him yet but, if he's
  willing, that would be my intention.
KING: Okay, your intention is to run and ask
  him to serve again?
CLINTON: Absolutely.
KING: And would you serve again if asked?
GORE: Well, I enjoy this job a great deal—

This is where my eyes probably glazed over. I'm sitting there with the president and the vice president of the United States and we're on international television, and what is foremost in my mind? I'm thinking to myself, "Al, stop with the bullshit already." Brando was right. We are all actors.

—And I count it as a privilege to have this
  learning experience and to be able to work
  for and with President Clinton. And you
  shouldn't have any doubt about that. But
  we're waiting on any formal announcements.

I understood what Vice President Gore was doing and with an answer like that I wished I hadn't even asked the question because there were hundreds of issues I wanted to get into with them, but this was a legitimate question and, unfortunately, a legitimate answer. We covered terrorism and attempts to determine if more than two men were involved in the Oklahoma City bombing. Clinton wanted to cut the eight years it takes to exhaust appeals in death penalty cases and find a way to make it a single appeal. The suspects, if convicted in the bombing, faced capital punishment. We covered Dole's recent attack on Hollywood for putting out too many violent films and Clinton said he agreed with a lot of what the now official candidate for the Republican presidential nomination was saying but added, there is a role for the media and the community and churches and business, and the issue should be handled in a way that brings sides together rather than dividing them further. It was a variation on a theme I was getting used to hearing and it began back in the '92 campaign, "I'm in the party of inclusion, not exclusion."

The time shot right past and before we closed the interview we took a call from Jamison, Pennsylvania. I can still hear the lady's words.

> CALLER: My question is . . . how frustrating is
> it for you to try and get your message out to
> the people when it seems like the opposing
> party is criticizing you constantly?
> KING: What do you make of the daily hate?
> There is a lot of hate in America.
> CLINTON: There is. And I would say to her I
> don't mind the daily criticism. What I don't
> like and don't agree with is the sort of
> atmosphere of negativism and cynicism . . .
> so I say to the lady it bothers me not to be
> criticized, but it bothers me there is an
> atmosphere that is more negative than
> positive. America should be more positive
> than negative.

During the interview, the Republican party bought an ad

on *Larry King Live* slamming the Clinton fiscal policy and

promise of a balanced budget within five years of being elected. I thought it was a brilliant move by the GOP and I expect we will see more such ads in years to come. And, of course, it came up in the questioning.

> KING: The Republican National Committee
> sent out a news release today saying you
> promised the American people you would
> offer a plan to balance the budget. Do you
> have such a plan?
> CLINTON: Well, as you know, I have said that
> I will work with the Republicans to balance
> the budget. And at the proper time I will
> offer how I think the best way to do it is,
> but I thought it was important after they
> won the election [1994] on a set of specific
> promises that they should have a chance to
> go and say how they think it should be
> done. Now you know what I think is wrong
> with their budget? I think that it cuts
> Medicare and other health programs too
> much.

Clinton's 1996 budget, after receiving the now standard DOA label when it went to Congress, was rejected and called for $200 billion deficits for the next few years. He said the deficit had been reduced by a billion dollars for the past three years and it just wasn't the right moment to come out with a statement announcing when the net would come to zero. I know budget issues are important and I know if there are bad numbers somewhere that fact will touch every American one way or another, but I think television shows talking about it are boring. On the radio show late at night I used to say to economists to just forget the actual number and tell me it's "higher" or "lower" or "not enough." That's as exact as I want to be. I used to see Lou Dobbs do his *MoneyLine* program at 6:30 on CNN, and sometimes would actually be in a nearby studio as he did it, and he could have been talking Swahili. But that's niche programming and it's a niche I'll never get into. The Republicans told the viewers the guest that night had no plan to make good on a balanced budget. He said it wasn't the time. My thought was, "By saying that, you have now doubled the pressure to *have* a plan." I understood that part and out of it all, I think I knew exactly what the important facts were.

Gore had told me off camera that Clinton could do a great Brando. All through the interview I was doing the "should-I-ask-it/shouldn't-I-ask-it" thing and with a few seconds left, well, let's just say asking about outyear tax projections wasn't going to allow appropriate time for a response.

> KING: You don't want to do a Brando close, do you?
>
> GORE: Just a handshake.
>
> KING: Just a handshake?
>
> CLINTON: We've enjoyed being on the show.
>
> KING: Oh, let me hear. President Clinton does Brando.
>
> CLINTON: No, no, no.
>
> KING: Do it once.
>
> GORE: You missed it.
>
> CLINTON: It's been great being on your show, Larry.
>
> KING: Thank you.

CLINTON: You got a real future in this
business.

When we were through everyone started laughing and that's when I realized there was the Brando imitation close I was asking him to do and then there was the Brando close which Brando had done right on my lips. I had flat-out missed what Clinton was telling me. If you want the truth, I'm glad he didn't do either one of them.

When the late-night radio show first called the Clinton White House Press Office to start what would be a weekly discussion about why the new president should speak to America as often as possible and to use radio as the medium to do so, the call was sent to a new department. Clinton had a person handling only radio interviews. When you looked at the numbers, it made sense. Talk radio formats had tripled from the time Clinton spoke in Atlanta in 1988 to his first term as president. Studies showed one out of every seven dollars in radio revenue came from the talk format. I thought a lot of it was loud and angry but people certainly tuned in to hear a host explain a point of view or, better yet, let a guest explain a point of view. Rush's callers always agreed with him and, quite frankly, the echo chamber got tiring to listen to after a while. Mutual's Jim Bohannon had a point of view and, many times, his guests and caller were on a different side of the street and it made, I think, for a healthy discussion. It was common for the White House to call my radio show during the day to offer Erskine Bowles (advisor to the president) or Robert Rubin (assistant to the president for economic policy) or Ira Magaziner (co-chair of the Health Care Task Force) to help get out whatever the message happened to be that particular day. The White House installed broadcast lines so the guest could do an interview with me or Bohannon and talk to the entire country while sitting in a studio down the hall from their office. We used it, as did all the other radio networks.

Three months after the interview with both Clinton and Gore, I did a special one-hour radio broadcast with the president from our Westwood One studios in Culver City, just outside Los Angeles and, even more important, just down the street from Culver Studios where scenes were shot for *Gone With the Wind* and *Citizen Kane*. The interview was the result of Westwood One chief executive officer Norm Pattiz telling the White House Bill Clinton gets the hell beat out of him every day on local radio, be it with Rush Limbaugh affiliates or conservative local talk show hosts, and all of it goes unanswered by the White House. Doing a one-hour national show, he argued, and taking calls from listeners and answering e-mail and faxes with more than three hundred affiliates, would be a smart move. It would get the message out and there would be no filter from a conservative host. Norm can be persuasive. The White House was persuaded.

Westwood One always reminds me of the *Starship Enterprise*. It has that quiet hum and the rooms are all filled with blue and red and white lights on control boards. Everywhere there's a digital clock telling you the time to the 100th of a second. You just get the feeling the room could take off if it hasn't already. It ain't easy to find either. I remember one night when Dom DeLuise insisted on driving himself over for an interview rather than take the limo offered by the radio show. And of course, he got lost. And with minutes to go before we went on the air, there was no sign of Dom. Then one of those white lights in the control room started flashing and the engineer picked it up. Dom was calling from his car. Dom didn't know where the hell he was. The engineer talked him through the turns and I walked out into the parking lot to watch as his car pulled in. He got out, looked at me, and said, "I feel like Doris Day in *Julie* when she was talked down by air traffic control and landed the airplane." We made it to the studio with forty-five seconds to go. Piece of cake. Dom could have stopped for coffee.

Clinton cut it closer. Blocks of Washington Boulevard were cordoned off, sharpshooters were on the Westwood One roof, and Culver City buses blocked the entrances to the large parking lot behind the building. I remember standing in the lobby just outside the studio looking at the digital clocks tell me the 100th of a second that was passing and, I gotta tell you, it made the wait all the worse. Always the producer, Norm suggested we put the president on by phone from his car. It made sense. And then, with thirty seconds to air, the limo with the presidential seal pulled into the driveway. Clinton was out the door immediately, so it was clear even he knew this was going to be close. He greeted Norm, posed for a few pictures, and then came into the studio while the theme was rolling. Bill Clinton is the guest who has cut it the closest out of all the guests I've ever had on the show. It was made all the worse by the stupid digital clocks telling me it was now 1:06:35 and three tenths. You just don't need to know those things.

Clinton said this was part campaign trip and part work-related. He had been in San Francisco meeting with business executives about how to get computers into schools and then how to train teachers to use the computers. And he was doing some fund-raising. But he wasn't going to say the words other than everyone knew he was going to run again but this just wasn't the right time. And I'm thinking to myself, what's this "the right time" routine? He wanted to wait until after the budget battle with the House because to announce now would make the entire spending plan partisan and, as a result, dead on arrival (again). I asked him about New Jersey senator Bill Bradley's decision to get out of Congress because he was disgusted (in total, fifteen senators said they weren't running again in 1996) and Colin Powell's statement from a few nights earlier that people right now were disgusted with both Republicans and Democrats.

> CLINTON: Larry, look at all of this. People are going to be faxing us, they're going to be e-mailing us, they're going to be doing all this stuff on the Internet. This is a hundred-year change period we're going through. And it's not surprising in a period like this that people would be looking around at all their options because they think there are so many balls up in the air.
>
> KING: So, therefore, come independent candidates and disfavor and people leaving politics?
>
> CLINTON: Yes. And not only that, if you go home at night you've got forty channels on television and they say, which would you rather have, three parties or two—you'd say three.

I got my first e-mail question. It appeared on my computer monitor, which was something I just couldn't get into no-matter, no-way, no-how. I used the same monitor taking phone calls and was comfortable but I still didn't trust it. And now an entire text appeared. It was from England and the listener wanted to know the president's view of the O.J. trial, since the jury was going to get the case within the next week. And as I read the question I kept thinking some guy with a computer on the other side of the world just typed it out and now it comes out of the radio with my voice. Clinton had it right. We were in a hundred-year cycle of upheaval and I was only sixty-two.

> CLINTON: I would hope neither the American
> people nor our friends in the United
> Kingdom would judge the American justice
> system entirely on this trial because the
> facts are so unusual. First of all the trial was
> televised, which I think contributed to the
> circuslike atmosphere and some of the
> developments.
> KING: You're opposed to televising?
> CLINTON: You run a serious risk when you do
> it in such a high-profile trial . . .
> KING: And as attorney general in—
> CLINTON: Arkansas
> KING: —did you ever have a televised trial?
> CLINTON: Never.

As he said this I thought about the O.J. Industry. I remember Lenny Bruce telling me thirty-plus years earlier that J. Edgar Hoover must have kissed the picture of John Dillinger every night before he went to bed. Otherwise, nobody would have known anything about the FBI director. And Lenny's theory, like all of Lenny's theories, held true today: If this trial wasn't on television, a lot of people wouldn't have jobs as pundits. I also thought Clinton was right. The question then becomes, So what do you do? Not cover it? Do you then say, no more televised trials? If you don't say that, then how do you decide which one is on TV and which one isn't?

We went to a commercial break and talked about his schedule and where he was headed next, and then he leaned in a little and asked, "Who you dating?"

"Nobody in particular," I said. "I get together with a few nice women. Cindy Garvey and I have dinner and Jo-Ellan Dimitrious, who is a guest for the Simpson trial, is a good friend. I like Marcia Clark's assistant Suzanne Chiles but the answer is nobody exclusive."

He smiled and nodded. "I admire your flexibility," he said.

I wanted to do some follow-up, but the clock was indicating I only had 4.365 seconds before we were back on the air. Still, I thought it was one of those comments all of us make from time to time that allow a momentary light into a usually dark area. I guess that's a non-Brooklyn way of saying I wasn't going to ask the question I wanted to ask.

The Trial of the Century came to a dramatic close a few days later. I was sitting with my producer, Wendy Walker Whitworth, and lifelong friend Asher Dan at Nate & Al's for a quick breakfast before going to work. The streets were empty. The restaurant was empty. In Los Angeles, as in every other city across the country, people were gathered in front of their televisions and radios.

The jury didn't spend a lot of time deliberating and, of course, each pundit on the air was drawing meaning into this fact. Now, had the jury spent nineteen days deliberating the pundits would have found meaning there as well. And we would have all listened. I had talked on the phone that day with Herb Cohen, who said, "I don't know what I'm going to do without being able to watch Judge Ito every day. It was a nice routine because as soon as they broke for lunch at noon in L.A., I could turn on Jerry Springer here in D.C. and have another hour of education." I knew as I sat and waited that every television was tuned to this moment across the country and the world. People later told me about being in Paris and watching CNN in their hotel rooms. It made me wonder if ESPN was gonna do a cut-in or if HBO would stop the 119th replay of *Norma Rae* and go live to the courtroom? I wasn't going to find out. Nobody knew the answer. In *Perry Mason* it always seemed he was gonna lose big-time and maybe then he'd go home with Della Street, but you always knew he was going to win. Not this time.

I think all of us will remember O.J.'s face as the first "not guilty" was read and then repeated on the second count. And that clip is replayed again and again whenever the story is of The Trial. I wonder, today, if an anchor will read an O.J. story in the year 2006 (and you know an anchor is going to do just that) and say, "Ladies and gentlemen, you've seen the video from October 1995 so many times, we've just decided to tell the story without it." A few years later we were going to see another video clip over and over of a woman with a beret and while it wasn't The Trial it was, to be blunt, a trial to go through. Call it a transition but I think we're going to see both tapes for many years to come before someone figures out a new way to tell a story that will always be told.

The verdict proved racism is quiet. White people thought O.J. should have been convicted and blacks believed he was innocent, set up by racists in the L.A. police. Racism erupts from time to time and this verdict created one such explosion, making us spend time looking at how it came about and whether any progress has been made since the last time. In fact Dominick Dunne was on during Verdict Night and said as much:

> It points it out vividly. I mean, and I think of all the kind of civil rights advancements of the last thirty years are all washed away. I think we are so polarized from each other now.

I agreed. And if the entire O.J. experience did nothing else, it showed us who we are. Or, it gave us a reason to talk, if only for a moment, about who we are.

I had been talking to both the prosecution and the defense throughout the trial (and not using Robert Shapiro's cell phone number anymore, I might add) hoping to get commitments they would come on the show as soon as possible following a verdict. The night after the verdict I had Johnnie Cochran in the studio. And prior to his appearance, the production staff had talked with him about bringing along the now free O.J. He was the guest to have. He had been silent throughout the nine months and now, as we told Cochran, he had a chance to talk directly to the public and he had an hour to do it. It was win-win. As a backup, Cochran was given an inside studio number and a password in the event O.J. was more comfortable with a phone call. Did I think he would show up in person? Probably not. Did I think he would make a phone call? Probably not. I figured it would become a book and if that's the direction he was going to go, the worst thing he could do right now would be an interview. The mystery element was essential.

There are guests I've had on that make me ask myself,

"What can't they tell me right now and how difficult is it to keep that inside?" Cochran was such a guest. As we sat in the Los Angeles studio I wondered about the conversations he'd had that day. He and Robert Shapiro had exchanged public words about Cochran's handling of the closing arguments. Shapiro, in an interview with Barbara Walters, said he wouldn't work with Cochran again because Cochran had played the race card all the way. Then Cochran had a news conference saying that wasn't the case at all. I was watching the verbal tennis match and wondering why the hell these two intelligent men didn't just pick up the phone, talk to each other, and work it out? Of course, the way it was going now made for good television. And the fact both were scheduled as guests back to back made it all the more interesting. But one issue we got into right away was based on Dominick Dunne's comments twenty-four hours earlier:

> KING: How do you react to the charges you set
> race relations back? Dominick Dunne was
> very vocal last night in saying that you,
> Johnnie Cochran, set racial relations back
> in this country.
> COCHRAN: . . . We have to discuss the
> differences, the things that divide us, the
> disparity in these polls, and why people see
> things differently. And then we need to do
> something about it. You know, Dr. King said
> that in America you promise such and such.
> Let's hold up a mirror to society. Here's
> what you promised, here is what you
> delivered. And there is a disparity.

Cochran, as I fully expected, didn't budge on his argument with Shapiro. I was looking forward to the next evening.

With about ten minutes left in the show we were in a commercial break when I heard the producer's voice tell me through my earpiece that O.J. was on the phone. I mentioned it to Johnnie, who gave me a smug smile. I wondered, as I had at the beginning of the show, if he had known all along and this was one of those things he just wasn't going to tell me. We decided to keep O.J. as long as possible and if the show went into the next hour, well, the show went into the next hour. I mean, what am I gonna say, "Well, O.J., we're out of time but I hope you'll come back one of these days and answer the question about how the blood got into your Bronco? Thank you and good night." The scary thing about it was I had worked with people in the business, not at CNN, who would have done just that.

When I heard O.J.'s voice my thoughts no longer were on what Johnnie Cochran couldn't tell me. In fact, at that moment, I didn't care what Johnnie Cochran couldn't tell me. I had another focus now. O.J. wanted to respond to a caller who had asked about Allan Park, the limo driver hired to pick up O.J. who testified he had seen a figure in the shadows outside the front door of O.J.'s house. Simpson said Park had seen him place his bags outside and then he went back inside. He said the prosecution had distorted the facts.

SIMPSON: There was no shadowy figure
coming down the driveway. That's what
Marcia Clark told you, that's not what
Allan Park told you.
KING: O.J., how would you describe yourself?
Relieved? Angry? What?

SIMPSON: A little bit of everything. I think
    my basic anger, and this is the last thing I'm
    going to say before I leave, my basic anger
    is these misconceptions. My basic anger is
    that people I've heard that have followed
    the case have heard experts say that this
    was the testimony today and that wasn't the
    testimony today. Marcia Clark told you that.
    Allan Park did not tell you that.
KING: All right, a couple of quick things, and
    I will let you go.
SIMPSON: No, I've got to go.

I was certain O.J. was dying to talk and I kept thinking
if I stay with it he'll start doing what he has made a living
doing. Didn't work.

The next morning I was greeted with the news O.J. and
I were going to do a pay-per-view special produced by Turner
Broadcasting in which he would answer all the questions. It
amazed me how something so wacko could get so much
mileage. And I kept getting called by newspapers and television and radio asking when it would happen. The answer
was, it wouldn't happen, never was going to happen, and I
don't know how it happened. And then I would get the
follow-up question, "Well, Larry, how did this get started?"
This was nuts. We were going down a road I didn't know
existed and I'm being asked how I got on the road in the
first place when I'm not even driving. I guess there are people with not enough to do. And so when Robert Shapiro
walked into the studio that evening, I said hello, shook his
hand, and said, "It ain't true," to head off any question about
doing a pay-per-view with O.J. Somehow, after nine months

147

of trial work and sixteen-plus months of O.J., I think Shapiro already knew the answer.

When I asked him about the Johnnie Cochran issue Shapiro wouldn't comment about the matter other than to say Cochran was wrong to equate the racism of detective Mark Fuhrman with the Holocaust. But he did offer a general view.

> KING: What—give it to us, your thoughts on race, this trial, and Johnnie Cochran.
>
> SHAPIRO: Okay. Race, I've always said, Larry, that race would not and should not be an element of this case. I stand by that. Why do I stand by that? O.J. Simpson was not acquitted of this case because he was black. I don't in my heart of hearts believe that for one moment.
>
> KING: Even though many Americans do believe it?
>
> SHAPIRO: Many Americans do believe that and that's why when I said we played the race card, that's what has happened, we have divided the blacks and the whites in an unnecessary way. The evidence in this case that was presented to twelve people not by pundits, not by spin, not by tabloids, in the court of law on every crucial element in this case, there is reasonable doubt, and in many cases, real doubt.

One thing was clear after that week: O.J. wasn't going away. Legally, he was facing a civil trial even though chances were good we wouldn't see it on TV. Socially and culturally, he was still in demand because Marcia Clark signed a $4 million book deal, Chris Darden signed a book deal, Kato Kaelin got a radio talk show, and Mark Fuhrman got a book deal. Greta Van Susteren and Roger Cossack were going to get their own television show. Johnnie Cochran was having discussions with Court TV. If you believe O.J., the killer or killers of his wife and Ron Goldman are still out there. If you don't believe O.J., he isn't serving any time. And if you do or don't believe him, O.J.'s name conjures up events having nothing to do with football and that ain't going away and that might be a conviction of a different kind. For months after The Verdict, we would do an O.J. story when there was a new issue to discuss. Coverage was one such issue, even though I think everyone in the business had been wondering if we had done too much since we first heard about the murders. Some years later I asked the sage extraordinaire Andy Rooney about it:

> KING: What did you think of the story?
> ROONEY: Well I was fascinated by it. I kept
>   hearing people say how overcovered it was.
>   I was interested by it. And you know one
>   group of columnists, newspaper columnists,
>   and radio commentators would report the
>   story and do it night after night. And then
>   there was a second group who would say it
>   was being overcovered. And then someone
>   would come along and complain about the
>   guy who says it's being overcovered. And it
>   was just one thing after another and I
>   thought the American public learned an

awful lot about our system of justice from
O.J.

O.J. called my producer, Wendy, about a year ago asking
to appear on *Larry King Live*. When he was asked if there
was anything new he wanted to add to the story, O.J. said
no, there wasn't. We didn't put him on. During that trial we
learned a lot about a lot of things and just a little of it was
about O.J. I remember saying to a New York cab driver who
had picked me up one afternoon that we had a "great hour
last night" talking about O.J. He turned to me at the light
at Sixth Avenue and 48th and said, "Yeah, well what about
the other twenty-three hours?" The guy had a point. I work
in a world of "going live to" whomever in wherever and "it's
happening now" and "at this moment" all the time, having
guests draw conclusions about what this minute means. It's
healthy, it makes us pay attention, and it suggests we can
learn something from that particular span of seconds or hours
about what has already happened and apply it to what might
happen in the days or weeks or years to come.

But here's the thing as Ross Perot likes to say: Maybe we
ought to be aware that all this instant analysis is only that
and nothing more? Maybe, in our never-ending need to understand what and where and who we are, there has to be
an element of time involved too? In Bensonhurst we used to
argue about ball scores and Roosevelt and whether the sixth-
inning catch by Sandy Amoros of a Yogi Berra line drive
smash hit was the fourth biggest play in Dodger history (it
was the first) while standing on the street in front of Sid's
Pants store. But someone always came back after an hour or
a day or a year saying "you know, I've been thinking . . ."
which, of course, started the argument all over again. The

O.J. trial did teach us but the lesson won't be complete until after we've all had time to reflect on the words just heard. Television gives us the chance to look at and hear and draw conclusions of "the now," but that doesn't mean all the "tomorrows" and "laters" will always go along with it.

Maybe it's always been that way. But maybe, because the five-hundred-channel universe is going faster and faster while a minute is still just sixty seconds, what we see today really *is* what we'll see tomorrow. In a time when anything goes, folks, it's possible.

CHAPTER SIX

The Mess-Age

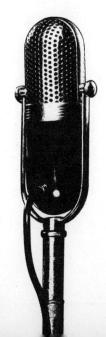

September 1995. It was Ross Perot who first introduced me to the idea of "an electronic town hall" where people could hear arguments on every side of an issue and cast a ballot via their television or computer or telephone as to how they wanted a congressman or a senator to vote. Certainly, it could become a way to elect a president. Whenever we televise a debate or when it can be heard on the radio or if it's the city council meeting on local access cable, it's an electronic town hall. There is no one way to do it and that's good. But this is a business where technology is far ahead of how it can be used, so I think Ross's idea will explode when we figure out the "what" of it. As for the "when," well, I'm not making any predictions.

The NAFTA debate was a town hall. Opposite sides were brought in, arguments for and against were made, and people who were affected by the issue, those in Mexico and

Canada as well as here, had the opportunity to call in and ask their own questions. My interview with Pete Rose, who wants to get into the Baseball Hall of Fame, was a town hall because he made his case and took questions from the audience all before the issue was decided by the Baseball Writers Association of America (who said no). Certainly, the Feinstein-Huffington debate was another one. On the eve of a key Senate vote on the balanced budget amendment I gathered the proponent-opponent-haven't-decided voices in the studio for an hour to have at it over the idea. This isn't new. In 1858, Abraham Lincoln and Stephen Douglas faced voters in seven debates throughout Illinois as they vied for the Senate. The electronic part is what continues to confound both viewer and participant. Producers would have been yelling at Lincoln to stand up straight, to avoid talking for an entire hour nonstop, to work on his voice, wear a different color, change the background—all of which had nothing to do with whether he would have been a good senator. He had to know his stuff. But I'll bet there was a guy watching the debate in Galesburg who said to his wife, "I'm going for Douglas, Lincoln just doesn't carry himself well." Knowing your stuff ain't enough. Never has been.

A version of the town hall took place in Orlando more than a year before the 1996 presidential election where Republican candidates for the GOP nomination got together in person and by satellite to debate issues and, maybe more important, introduce themselves to a public that doesn't really pay a lot of attention to them until a month or so before their particular state's primary. In the case of Florida, a straw poll was going to be held the following day and all GOP eyes were, for this moment, focused here. I had Alan Keyes, Pat Buchanan, and Lamar Alexander on stage at the Orange

County Convention Center, and in the Washington studio or in our Capitol Hill studio I had Phil Gramm, Bob Dole, Richard Lugar, Arlen Specter, and Robert Dornan, all members of Congress embroiled in the budget battle with the White House and, in many cases, with each other. Steve Forbes was in Washington as well. Bob Dole was tending to the business of the Senate and arrived late.

We went for two hours and, if I had the chance to do it over again, I'd ask to have all the candidates in one place. The Orlando guests were jumping in on comments made by those in Washington and it became (I'm gonna be diplomatic here) lively. It confounded the participants and, in this case, also the moderator. We are still learning, which is why there is always a debate about debates before there is a debate (location, format, questions from audience or not, and so on). The electronic town hall is, and always will be, a work in progress.

As we went on the air, Colin Powell had just announced he wasn't going to be a candidate for president in 1996. Everyone but Pat expressed interest in Powell as a running mate. "I want him in the church," Pat said, "but we're not going to make him the pope the first time he walks into the church." It was a good line and after the debate I worried if an ability to fire back a good line or, for that matter, an ability to just be good on television are reasons a person could be president. The answer is yes. That makes one ask: If a person is bad on television, can they be president? The answer is probably no. By the way, Bob Dole won the straw poll the next day.

Another variation on Ross's idea had taken place a few weeks earlier following the assassination of Israeli prime minister Yitzhak Rabin. I was interviewing then Likud party leader

Benjamin Netanyahu, who had attended the funeral that same day, about the resulting political conflicts in the country. The Labor and Likud parties went at each other constantly (sound familiar?) and I asked Netanyahu if he was willing to appear on the show with Labor leader Shimon Peres. He agreed to the idea and offered a variation on Ecclesiastes: "There is a turn for every season." I was convinced this could have a healing effect on the Israeli people or, if nothing else, allow each side to hear the other's voice. After all, you can't listen if you're talking.

During that same evening I had also done an interview with Nixon secretary of state Henry Kissinger, who was a major player in earlier peace talks between Egypt and Israel brokered by the United States. Henry, however, was in Shanghai, where live satellite feeds had never before been tried because television facilities didn't exist. We literally had to build them, rushing a studio to completion as the show went on the air. Kissinger made history again in this first live international broadcast. That fact alone made me think maybe this television business can have some kind of role in getting people who normally don't talk to start doing just that. This too was a beginning. The technology connecting Washington, D.C., with China was allowing the people in both places to have a conversation that, otherwise, wouldn't have occurred. It was more proof, as if I need more proof, of how cold wires, or whatever it is that happens with satellites, can warm the connections between countries if human beings will only allow it. So with Kissinger it was being used for warmth between Shanghai and the United States and with Netanyahu and Peres it was being used to bring a different kind of warmth to an already heated situation.

That same week I interviewed PLO chairman Yasser

Arafat, who couldn't attend Rabin's funeral out of concerns for his safety. We had done a number of face-to-face tapings including one just after the Middle East peace accord had been signed on the White House lawn between Rabin and Arafat. Never before had I seen so much security around one person as I did with the Palestinian leader. But when I got through the searches and waiting and paperwork and questions, Arafat had a great sense of himself. He told me whatever happens is the result of destiny and nothing else. If he is meant to be killed, he will be killed. I came away from both interviews with Arafat wondering if technology could advance diplomacy. And I concluded it couldn't if the opposing sides only showed up on screen instead of talking from the heart.

But there's a catch to all of this. And Bosnia is where it became the most pronounced. In a true electronic town hall, and in this case we're talking countries rather than cities, the audience has to have a chance to learn why the issues are important to them. In Bosnia, we kept referring to the fact that it had the potential of being another Vietnam, which it did, and that these sides had been fighting each other for centuries, which they had. Sort of makes one wonder what's to gain by getting involved. We did a lot of shows about this and through it all my biggest problem was trying to pronounce the names of guests. Bosnia's prime minister, Haris Silajdzic, was with me in the Washington studio one night urging that the arms embargo be lifted. It was an international town hall because not only was Silajdzic talking to Americans but he was talking to the French, the British, and the Germans to urge their support as well. Before going on the air I said his name over and over to make sure I got it right. And when the moment came I intentionally slowed

159

down and got through it. I could see he was smiling. So my first question was, "Did I get it right?"

"This time, it's right. Good, Larry," he said in perfect English.

I'll tell you this: For the rest of the half hour, he was identified as "the prime minister." I used a lot of titles in the Bosnia shows.

While I was trying to pronounce proper nouns without vowels, budget talks in plain English between the White House and Congress broke down, which resulted in the furlough of more than 800,000 government employees. Republicans were going all out to have Clinton agree on a seven-year spending plan, while the White House said the elements in the plan were too draconian. In other words, it was the same argument as always; just different words. Democrats faced off with Ronald Reagan on the budget all the time but it never reached this point. During the threats, which are an essential part of how America legislates, I never thought a shutdown of government operations would actually happen, and so when it did I figured we were looking at a one-day event to make the point, and then we'd get on with it.

On the second night of the six-day closing, I had House Budget Committee Chairman John Kasich and Senator Kent Conrad in the studio. If there ever was a moment for an electronic town hall, it was now. I have known both Kasich and Conrad for a long time and I was looking forward to seeing them and hearing the arguments but I wasn't ready for the insanity that took over the hour.

Let me put it this way: If you're going to shut a government down, then there ought to be more to it than what I heard. Kasich quoted the *Washington Post* as supporting his position, while Conrad said the *Wall Street Journal* favored his position. I'm listening to this thinking "so what?" Kasich said the Office of Management and Budget uses numbers favorable to the White House because OMB director Alice Rivlin is appointed by the president. Conrad said the Congressional Budget Office numbers are wrong also because its director is appointed by the House, so he wanted a panel of experts on economic forecasts to sit down and put out the real numbers. Both Kasich and Conrad believed what they were saying but I still couldn't fathom this as a cause to shut down a government. If Thomas Jefferson could have been brought into the studio that night and given a seat off camera to watch this I'm positive he'd have first said, "Larry, I think I screwed up big-time. You got a quill I can borrow and a copy of the Constitution?" His next remark would have come after looking around the studio: "What's all this stuff?" It was Senator Ernest Hollings who once told me during a commercial break when another debate was raging that what Congress does is like making sausage; it ain't a pleasant thing to watch. He was right.

> KING: Why don't the two of you agree?
> KASICH: Well, it's going to get down to
> people wanting to settle it. Because if we
> can settle it, we're going to have to give
> and take once we've defined the parameters
> in which we are going to debate.
> KING: Do you agree with that?
> CONRAD: Yes, and I will just say to John, why
> can't we agree? Let's not use CBO, let's not
> use OMB, let's get a panel of experts—
> KING: He's not going to agree.

> KASICH: We're going to do it for the kids and
> we're going to hang tough.

I was never so glad for a show to come to an end as I was that evening. This was a time when the electronic town hall would have put Congress and the White House on the spot to explain what was happening. For instance, had the television viewer been asked, "Would you like to shut down the government for six days so someone can make a point?" the answer would have been a resounding "Are you crazy?" or a variation thereof. In fact, had the viewer been asked, "How about just shutting it down for a day?" the answer would have been the same, with a few four-letter words as well.

Of course, there could have been the most electronic of all town halls available so that each side could make its case to the public, but the issue wasn't going to be decided unless the White House and Congress actually talked to each other. So what was going on had nothing to do with technology. Amazingly, wacko time wasn't over when the furloughed workers went back to their jobs because one week before Christmas the government shut down again, this time for twenty days. I watched C-SPAN and listened to the one-minute speeches going on in the House, which is what they do before any business is conducted, and realized my head was going to explode. I picked up the clicker and found a three-week-old soccer game in Spanish. I don't understand soccer and I don't speak Spanish but that hour made more sense to me than anything going on in English that day. It was to be, unfortunately, a premonition of things to come.

*   *   *

Bob Dole had trouble throughout the 1996 campaign getting his "message" across to voters. It was most obvious after Bill Clinton's 1996 State of the Union Address in which the president declared "the era of big government is over" and was able to do so in less time than his PBS-like marathon address of a year earlier. But when Dole gave the Republican response, there was no "there" there. Dole wasn't connecting. I didn't see or hear anything resembling a message. And yet, this was the same guy who was the most frequent guest on my television show, and in every appearance he came across with purpose and direction and did both with the sharpest wit on Capitol Hill. But he lost the New Hampshire primary to Pat Buchanan by one percentage point. Dole came back in the March primaries and by April it was a done deal that he and Clinton would face each other in November. At issue was the country's direction and road map for the next four years and I just wasn't spending a lot of time saying "gee I oughta watch this Dole speech or Clinton speech or hear Perot talk to his people." Unlike 1992, there was no uncertainty about the major players prior to the election. And when that happens, it's difficult for the voter, and even more difficult for the nonvoter, to care.

But there was an evening when I had on former George Bush campaign official and now CNN Crossfire cohost Mary Matalin along with Tabitha Soren of MTV, who was covering the campaign. The most exciting thing going on was that Tabitha had just interviewed Bob Dole, which not only was a good move for her but was an even better move for Dole. He was taking his cues from four years earlier when Clinton visited Arsenio Hall to reach potential voters who otherwise wouldn't make the effort to tune in a Dole interview on CNN.

MATALIN: His underneath numbers are very
squishy.

KING: He just went up.

MATALIN: That's the top numbers. But
everything under there is soft.

SOREN: Well, don't you think even discussing
this at this point is a little premature?

MATALIN: Thank you.

SOREN: And pointless.

KING: The whole thing pre— Well, yeah.

SOREN: Clinton, where was he in February
four years ago? He was in Gennifer Flowers
Land, you know?

MATALIN: Good answer. You're good.

KING: Well, you go beyond, Tabitha—it's the
work. Tabitha was once an intern at CNN.
When you go beyond thirty years old, you
learn that—

SOREN: Do you have to talk about only polls
and predictions?

KING: What's there to talk about?

SOREN: Well, what about the issues? I mean
you just can't, you can write off the
populace for not voting, when you are not
doing your job explaining what we've been
talking about.

She changed the conversation for the rest of the hour,
although I will admit by the time the show ended we were
still predicting primary outcomes. I have always appreciated
the high road but you always have to take a lower-elevation
route to get there.

The events of 1996 made me think of an interview I'd had one night in the radio studio with Barry Goldwater. Although at the time he was recovering from hip surgery and walked with two canes and was frail physically, Goldwater's spirit was sharp. He told me of his plans for a presidential run in 1964 and of a discussion he'd had with the man who would be his opponent: John F. Kennedy:

> I went to Jack's office and he wasn't there so I just
> sat down in his chair and lit a cigar. Jack comes in
> from the private bathroom, sees me and says, "You
> want that to be your chair in '64?" and I said that's
> my plan and he sits down in the chair in front of the
> desk. I told him I was going to run in 1964 and I
> have a few ideas about how we oughta do it.
> Kennedy looks at me and says, "We?" I said why
> don't we both use the same airplane and fly together
> to cities and debate each other? What sense does it
> make for both of us to fly to the same city to do the
> same thing? Kennedy looked at me and said it was a
> good idea.

For just a moment I wondered (that word again) what it would be like for Bill Clinton and Bob Dole to meet a few times every month in a different city and debate each other. For that matter I was wondering why Clinton and Dole or Clinton and Gingrich didn't just set aside an hour a week to break bread together. It was historian Doris Kearns Goodwin who once told me how Franklin Roosevelt would argue all day with Republicans and then play poker with the same guys in the evening. I didn't know the answers to the disconnect I was feeling but I was wishing Clinton and Gingrich would sit down for a game of five-card draw every now and then. During the government shutdown, Clinton had called Dole and suggested they fly together to Florida and talk about a solution. So it made me think how Clinton and Dole would be handling their campaigns today had JFK lived for another run at the job.

There had been stories about Kennedy and women. Goldwater was on just after the Gary Hart episode with Donna Rice; an affair which forced the Colorado senator out of a run for the 1988 Democratic presidential nomination. I asked him about it. He gave me one answer on the air: Hart had made a mistake; and then he gave me another answer off the air during a commercial break. As soon as I had said Hart's name, Goldwater began shaking his head:

> Hart? He didn't have it. All these guys want to act
> like Jack Kennedy and they aren't in Jack's league.
> We all knew about the women but nobody ever
> talked like they do now. I remember going to the
> White House for a meeting with him just after a trip
> I made to West Berlin. Jack says, "You had an affair
> with an assistant to the ambassador, didn't you?" It
> was true. He told me he wanted to have an affair
> with her but couldn't because he was too visible as
> president. So I asked how he found out and Jack
> looks at me without any smile at all and says, "Barry,
> I'm the president of the United States."

I had interviewed Judith Exner about her claims of an affair with Kennedy, which she says began during the 1960 campaign and continued after he won the White House. She said people looked the other way then. We'd have reported

Kennedy's affairs and we'd have reported Goldwater's affair were they running today. We'd have known later on that Goldwater voted for Hubert Humphrey rather than Richard Nixon and we'd have brought on the pundits to discuss whether that fact alone could derail his bid for the GOP nomination. It would have been one hell of a campaign and the race would have had a record turnout. That would have been an electronic town hall to see and hear. But it was only the stuff of words now.

I was in Los Angeles one afternoon watching ESPN when the phone rang. I answered it to hear the words, "Larry, it's Marlon." The voice was familiar so, of course, I said my lines. "Marlon who?" We agreed it was time for another interview, this time in the studio. He wanted to talk about racism and the recent beatings in Riverside, California, of immigrants by police. Somehow I didn't think he called to talk about *On the Waterfront*.

I was really looking forward to being with Mr. B. again, in part because this guy is so much fun and also in part because it was a break from politics and O.J. stories. But when we went on the air, it was a serious Brando in the studio. We talked about violence and he said it was a part of being human. He said racism is the result of fearing differences in people and it isn't going to stop until we try to understand the differences. That is the tough part. Some people never even get to that point. The conversation moved quickly and soon we were talking about the ethnic grouping of people. And that's when Brando offered the example of Hollywood casting minorities in stereotypical roles. It's an issue to which Jews need to pay attention:

They should have a greater sensitivity about the issue
of people who are suffering because they've
exploited—we've seen the nigger we've seen the
greaseball, we've seen the chink, we've seen the slit-
eyed dangerous Jap, we've seen the wily Filipino.
We've seen everything but we've never seen the kike.

"Hollywood," he went on to say, "is run by Jews. It's
owned by the Jews. I will be the first one to praise the Jews
honestly and say thank God for the Jews." As we came out
of the first commercial break I decided to do one quick
follow-up question for clarification and then return to the
Riverside beatings.

> KING: We're back with Marlon Brando. He
>   does want to clear up his criticism of Jewish
>   people who are in positions of power in
>   Hollywood—
> BRANDO: I don't want to clear it up. I
>   think—
> KING: You don't want people to think that
>   you're—
> BRANDO: I think that, no, the Jews have
>   the— They know perfectly well what their
>   responsibilities are.

I was concerned his words could be blown up out of pro-
portion had someone tuned in late, so I figured a quick recap
would put the issue to rest. It was a quicker recap than I expected and we were off to more discussion about civil rights.
I never thought the exchange was going to create a problem

for anyone. Another prediction from me and you can guess where it went.

As I had come to expect, the hour seemed to contain only seven minutes. When we were done, I shook his hand— no Brando close this time—and told him I was going to dinner with some friends and would he like to join us? Brando agreed and an hour later we were sitting at the Eclipse in Beverly Hills singing "Some Day When I'm Old and Gray" among other tunes. Two guys from my old neighborhood, Sid Young and Asher Dan, were there, along with *Larry King Live* executive producer, Mary Gregory, and Jo-Ellan Dimitrius. Everyone at the table was laughing and trying to keep up with the songs and the stories and the verbal barbs from Marlon. It was one of those times when everything clicks. There was no talk about the remarks he had made during the show. Around midnight I left to go home and walked out the door to find the paparazzi gathered to get a photo of Marlon. There were no questions about the interview.

At 1:00 A.M. the telephone rang. I had been asleep for almost thirty minutes.

"Larry, it's Marlon."

I had the lines ready to go and we went through the routine.

"Let's go to Mexico," he said. Marlon had lined up a plane and the entire table I'd left earlier was at his house. Everyone was going. He told me Sean Penn was coming along too.

"I don't know— I, it's late—"

He told me where to be and at what time and after I hung up the phone I asked myself, Why Mexico? Why not the Santa Monica Pier? Why not just stay right where we are? How did I get talked into this? Did I get talked into this? What the hell are we gonna do in Mexico? That's when the phone rang.   169

"Larry, it's Marlon."

No, I didn't do it this time. The trip was off. Penn couldn't find his passport. I thanked him for the call and lay back on my pillow. I was grateful for what I had but more grateful for what Sean Penn didn't have.

The interview with Mr. B. had aired on a Friday. When I turned on the television Monday morning all hell was breaking loose. And I was dumbfounded. A black swastika had been painted on Brando's star on the Walk of Fame (as if Brando would care about a star in the first place). The Jewish Defense League was furious and said Brando had now stereotyped the Jews as owning everything. Producers and directors were on camera saying Brando's films should be boycotted and I stood there wondering how this could have happened. CNN switchboards in Atlanta, Washington, New York, and Los Angeles were getting bombarded with telephone calls. I thought the Brando interview had been good, and even though I had been concerned someone catching a one-minute segment of the exchange could come away with the wrong impression, if they saw the full segment on Jews in Hollywood it would have allayed any doubt. But, obviously, I was wrong once again.

Dan Quayle had been on the show years earlier and talked about abortion and I thought that was a nonissue as well. As I learned and, certainly as Quayle learned, and now as Brando learned, what happens in the studio is different from what happens in the living room. What one sees depends, I guess, on where one sits.

Brando called me a few days later and we compared notes. He said he didn't know how this happened and he had met with Rabbi Marvin Heir of the Wiesenthal Center to explain his position. After I hung up I realized the electronic town hall that had been occupying my mind of late isn't going to work if people watch it and come away with an entirely different take of what is said. Of course, this has been happening since Cro-Magnon did drawings of an animal on a cave wall and another Cro-Magnon asked what's with the cloud paintings?

During this time, Bob Woodward, who had written about Hillary Clinton's fascination with the former first lady, Eleanor Roosevelt, reported that Hillary and Eleanor talked to each other using spiritual guide Jean Houston as a medium. Mrs. Clinton wouldn't agree to an interview but Houston came into the studio to talk, in general, about how she communicates with the dead. I have never been a fan of this stuff but I'm always willing to learn. I'd had the psychic Char on my radio and television shows, who would talk to callers and tell them their deceased relative was okay, but she had also worked with police using her abilities to find lost children, so it sure seemed like something was going on. Still, I was dubious. Jean Houston offered to help me get past the doubt and said "select someone to talk to." I picked Arthur Godfrey, who died in 1983 and was the man responsible for getting me into the radio business in the first place. The idea was Godfrey would speak to me though the connection Houston was able to set up.

"Well, Arthur, this is Larry. What are your perceptions of broadcasting today?"

Out of nowhere I started answering my question. "I would never have dreamed of satellites." I agreed with that. I would have never dreamed of them either. Houston urged me to ask a follow-up question.

"What advice do you have for my career?"

"Take the show on the road more often. You need to touch people more. Go overseas."

"Am I doing okay with it so far? Anything else I should change?"

Godfrey liked the show. The answers came automatically to me. I didn't disagree with anything he said. Did I think I was talking to the great broadcaster? Well, if there is a some-place else, and if I had lived my entire life working in radio and the early days of television, I'd probably want to get back on the air too. Sometimes, you gotta work with what you have available.

If timing is everything, Ross Perot's announcement he was back in the running just before the Republicans con-vened in San Diego was all one could ask for. He didn't do it the way he did four years earlier, but Ross has never been predictable. He came back to the same studio and spent an hour fielding questions from all over the world. I asked him if he was going to be in for the long run this time and as I said the words, I could tell he wasn't enjoying the moment.

> I don't want to get into that. The point is, can
> someone stop and take a few minutes and look and
> see what I've done night and day for the past five
> years?

I believed him. But it was frustrating. The questions de-served better answers than he was giving. Ross has always been a complicated man. I was certain he wasn't trying to duck anything being thrown his way. What I don't think he understood was that the 1992 race with Perot was charac-terized by a few moments and he expected everyone to view those moments at the same level as all the other moments.

It ain't gonna happen because (1) we don't view anything else that way and (2) we don't have enough time to do it.

Ross came on to do a second interview that summer, which took away any lingering thoughts I might have had about his being complicated. When the "members," as they were now being called, elected him to be the Reform party candidate over former Colorado governor Dick Lamm, Perot announced he was going to take matching federal funds. I asked him about it. "In talking to our members, they wanted to put some skin in the game. We're asking them to make small contributions. We don't take any giant contributions from PACs at all." He had talked about wanting "skin" from supporters back in 1992 too. It was a good line and it captured the idea that we are in this together. Perot was bothered, though, by the fact that out of more than a million ballots sent out, only about fifty thousand were returned. There didn't seem to be much skin in this campaign.

Two days later and just before the Republican convention was to take place in San Diego, Bob and Elizabeth Dole came on to talk about why he wanted to be the next president of the United States. Dole was still having trouble in the polls with women, which was why Mrs. Dole was with him. He had been going nonstop since announcing his candidacy in April, and to show he was serious about the job he wanted, Dole had resigned as Senate majority leader and as senator from Kansas. He discarded the blue pinstripe suit, white shirt, and tie, replacing them with dress slacks and a sports coat and looking absolutely uncomfortable. But this was a way to say, without using the words, that he wasn't a part of the Washington scene anymore. Of course the pinstripes were back when he came on the set that night.

Dole announced on the air he would have Congresswoman Susan Molinari deliver the keynote address in San Diego, a total surprise to all the pundits as well as Molinari. It was another attempt to bring in the essential woman vote, or the "soccer moms," which I had first thought was the result of women getting bored with what they saw on TV and getting hooked on the same Spanish games I had been watching. But Molinari supported abortion rights, which was an issue that plagued the campaign and the party because of the far right's insistence that being against abortion was the litmus test in order to be a candidate for president or vice president, and the fact the party had a keynoter outside of the litmus test wasn't going to make Dole's attempts to build an inclusive party any easier. It was a gutsy move on Dole's part, who made the point that Republicans can't be a one-issue party. Molinari was having dinner with her husband at a restaurant in New York when the *Larry King Live* staff reached her by cell phone. I thought it strange Dole hadn't even called her for a heads-up but I was glad he didn't. From her table Molinari accepted the offer on the air. Looking back, which I do a lot now, it was the only spontaneous thing to happen during the entire campaign.

Dole had been dogged with two other issues: He had not accepted an invitation to speak to the NAACP convention and realized, very quickly, that had been a mistake. His campaign staff cited "scheduling conflicts," which I think was believed by, possibly, two people in Montauk. He was criticized by Jack Kemp of Empower America on a CNN program for not understanding the importance of making the speech. A week later, Kemp became Dole's running mate. The other issue was smoking. Dole had made the mistake of rambling in an interview when asked about tobacco's effect on the body and when given a chance to hit the ball right out of the park, he chose instead to strike out by saying he wasn't a doctor. I asked him if he could have given a better answer, which was another opportunity to hit it out of the park.

> It's not good for you. My brother had emphysema.
> One of the major contributing causes to his death
> was smoking. My father had a problem. He stopped.
> So it's not good for you. It's bad for your health.
> Don't do it.

Dole paused as he said the last words. I could see his mind was at work. He took a breath and started in again. "Now, having said that—"

Out of nowhere Elizabeth Dole's hand came to a rest on her husband's forearm. "That's it," she ordered.

Dole leaned back, smiled, and said, "That's it."

This happened a number of times during the hour and by the end of the show we were all sharing the humor in it. I asked Dole if he would select Supreme Court justices on the basis of their ideological beliefs and he answered, "I'll have litmus tests for all judges. I want them to be tough on crime. I want them to interpret the Constitution, not try to amend it." That brought out Mrs. Dole's hand on the forearm again.

"Not legislate from the bench," she added.

Just before the interview we had done the small talk about "how is it going?" and "where are you going?" and Dole told me he enjoyed the campaign and meeting voters. I mentioned how it's important to love what you do because it usually makes you do whatever it is even better. And I told him of the last time I was with Clinton in the Oval Office, before an interview, and how he talked about how lonely a job it is to be president but added, "Even my bad days are good

175

days." Dole looked down for a second. "I'm in trouble," he said. Then he looked at me. "If your bad days are good days it's tough to beat a guy like that."

The story of the Republican convention in San Diego was television. It had been designed for the TV audience so all the big names (Gerald Ford, Colin Powell, Kay Bailey Hutchison, Nancy Reagan) were slated to give their speeches within the hour the networks would provide coverage. It was choreographed-produced-packaged—and absolutely boring. Ted Koppel pulled out his *Nightline* crew and went back to New York saying there was no news to be found. He was right. There wasn't any hint of surprise, much less news, anywhere. The conventions had become four days of controlled events. Never would one hear a discouraging word. Never would one hear anything newsworthy. It was all Julie Andrews in a field on a sunny day singing "The hills are alive" and it got old after the first thirty-seven seconds. TV producers had been hired to make the program television-friendly and in doing so had made it impossible to watch. It was an infomercial that kept saying "wait, there's more" and you'd wait and nothing would happen. We had come a long way since George Mc-Govern's 3:00 A.M. acceptance speech at the Democratic convention in 1968 but it was the wrong way. In terms of news and national importance, 1968 was far ahead of 1996. CNN by its nature had to be there and cover it and I did interviews with party leaders but there was zero to talk about.

And the Democrats did the same thing the following week in Chicago. They still weren't able to start anything on time so at least there was some consistency. This too was a pre-produced, in-unity-we-sing, phony gathering of delegates covered by just as many journalists wearing the standard khaki vests. And the boredom wasn't just on the convention floor with the cheese heads. Ratings were in the cellar (only 12 percent of all televisions turned on were tuned to the conventions). It made me wish for a second ballot. Television had made democracy boring and I wondered if this was a vision of things to come; sort of a Ghost of Conventions Future? In fact the only "interesting" event in the Chicago convention took place far outside Chicago. Clinton's pollster, Dick Morris, had been using the services of a hooker and had resigned the job so as not to hurt the campaign. The story first appeared in the tabloid the *Star*. It started the questions: "Does this one event symbolize how the Clinton White House operates?" "If this goes on with pollsters then where else does it occur?" "Were any national security issues compromised?" The story came out on the day Clinton was going to deliver his acceptance speech. In 1992, on the day he was going to do the same thing, there was another story out there: Ross Perot had quit the race. And so this trend became a story too. I love Greektown and I love the lakefront and I love Michigan Avenue but not as much as I loved getting out of Chicago that year.

The electronic town hall idea was the good thing to come out of the 1996 race. Throughout October I hosted a number of issue-oriented programs in various cities that permitted the audience in the hall and the audience at home to weigh in on points being made. There was a lot of healthy back-and-forth, which should become a part of any future president's routine. Clinton and Dole held two debates watched by fewer people than the three-way race of four years earlier. Clinton did few, if any, interviews. It was clear the campaign decided to coast through controlled events rather than do live call-ins. The issue before the pundits during the last days of the campaign was by how many percentage points

177

Dole would lose the popular vote. After the election, Bob Dole told me "the best man lost." Had television won the election for one candidate and lost the election for other candidates? Absolutely not. Did the best man win? Beats me.

Despite the gimmicks and the vacuum and the never-ending attempts to make the campaign nothing more than a great big video with scripted words, 1996 was a pivotal election year. Every expert, every pundit, every politician I've talked to has said we shouldn't do it like that again.

In these times where anything goes, we now had an idea or two of where we didn't want to go. That leaves a lot of territory. And I figured since Bill Clinton was now a lame duck, it would be a quiet second term.

NOVEMBER 5, 1996

1996 Voting age population:	195,511,000
1996 Registration to vote:	146,211,960
1996 Turnout to vote:	96,456,345
Percentage of voting age who voted:	38.8 *lowest since 1924*
Popular vote for Bill Clinton:	45,628,667 (379 electoral votes) 50%
Popular vote for Bob Dole:	37,869,435 (159 electoral votes) 41%
Popular vote for Ross Perot:	7,874,283 (0 electoral votes) 9%

Source: Federal Election Commission

CHAPTER SEVEN

"Lewinskied"

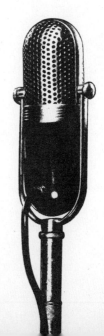

January 21, 1998. I'm on the treadmill in my home with the clicker in one hand, *USA Today* on a stand in front of me, and ESPN on the television. I'm listening to the Super Bowl hype and decide, after three seconds, there's got to be more going on in the world. So I tune to the Weather Channel because this is the day Pope John Paul arrives in Cuba and I'm curious if he's going to have to endure the Havana heat and humidity.

The pope and I are of different tribes, but he is a person with whom I could do business. Whenever I'm asked to name people I'd like to interview some day, the list begins with God (first question: Did you have a son because a lot is riding on the answer?), Hitler (How do you define evil?), and Pope John Paul II (What do you say to the Saddam Husseins of the world?). My interest in the pope was increased all the more when the Vatican announced he would travel to Cuba in early 1998 and meet with Fidel Castro who, thirty years earlier, had banned, among many other things, Catholic schools in the country. In addition, the pope was vocal about America's economic sanctions against Cuba and was a constant proponent for their removal. It has always seemed to me that sanctions hurt the people most in need of help and the despots to whom the sanctions are directed don't care about the people in the first place, which is why they have the job of despot. On a larger scale, talking is more productive than not talking. The United States has taken the no-talk side of the street and the way Castro sees the world hasn't changed one iota.

The Weather Channel told me John Paul II was going to face 80 degree temperatures, which got me going all the more. We don't talk to Cuba but we get an hourly temperature. I hit the clicker thinking a show from Cuba would be fantastic and it was something I was going to bring up at the next production meeting, even though I'm never invited to the production meetings. I went to CNN and watched the anchor say, "Once again, today's *Washington Post* is reporting Independent Counsel Kenneth Starr is investigating whether President Clinton told a White House intern to lie about an affair she had with him." CNN went to a commercial and my treadmill stopped.

The clicker was in motion, moving to Imus on MSNBC (who was in a commercial) to ESPN, which was now talking about the last 185 years of Green Bay and Denver contests and, probably to this day, has yet to mention Bill Clinton won the election in 1992. I clicked over to *Good Morning America*, which was doing an interview with a correspondent in Cuba, and then I went to Matt Lauer as he said, "This is

Today on NBC," which is the standard cue before, yeah, you guessed it. I was all dressed up with nowhere to go.

CNN came out of its commercial and did the story. President Clinton was being accused of having an affair with a twenty-one-year-old intern named Monica Lewinsky. She had been taped, without her knowledge, talking about her relationship with the president by a colleague at the Pentagon named Linda Tripp and that tape had been given to Independent Counsel Kenneth Starr, who had been hired to investigate Whitewater. The country had been through Clinton's alleged extracurricular activities before and my first thought was the same as the rest of the country: not again. My second thought was Newt Gingrich must be doing back flips right now.

Earlier that week, Clinton had testified for six hours about his relationship with Paula Jones, a former Arkansas state employee who accused then-Governor Clinton of suggesting oral sex in a Little Rock hotel room. This was serious stuff because it implied not only a disturbing pattern of behavior with women, but a classic case of what shouldn't occur between supervisor and employee. And as was true with Gennifer Flowers, it was he said–she said again. I felt as though the country was living the theme of *Groundhog Day*, where the same thing keeps happening over and over. The only difference was the movie was a comedy. This wasn't.

Within the first minute of hearing the word "intern" I knew we were heading full blast into the frenzy, if we hadn't arrived already. That's when the phone rang. It was Wendy saying we were going to change the guest lineup around tonight but she was going to keep Israeli prime minister Benjamin Netanyahu because he was meeting with Clinton today. I would tape him in a few hours and I already knew my first question would have absolutely nothing to do with discussions about giving up land to the Palestinians while protecting Israeli security. After I hung up the phone I looked again at the television screen. There was video of Clinton walking from *Marine One* on the South Lawn. "You're finished," I said to the picture.

Exactly three hours later I was in the studio talking with the Israeli prime minister via satellite. He and I had known each other since his days as Israel's ambassador to the United Nations. And I remember Netanyahu and his wife drove me to the airport after my first visit to Israel in 1991. I couldn't get over the idea that when this political force said "I'll take you to the airport" that's exactly what he meant: He drove me to the airport. But even before I had met him and long before he became Israel's head of state, Netanyahu had endured coverage of the fact he too had had an affair. At the time it was called "Bibigate." He knew the first question.

> KING: You spent some time with the president, were with him late last night, and you yourself have occasionally had the stories come down about Prime Minister Netanyahu. How has the president reacted to all of this?
>
> NETANYAHU: He didn't react at all. He was absolutely businesslike. We talked over three hours in two successive meetings, including one late into the night yesterday. It was right on target, focused, businesslike, very nimble and very creative. I think he's doing his job.

KING: When you visit a country and then
   something like this happens—it can happen
   anywhere to any visiting head of state—are
   you put in kind of a difficult position when
   a story is breaking that is tabloidish in
   nature?
NETANYAHU: . . . I have to tell you that
   usually you keep a level head with these
   things. And my rule in life and in political
   life in particular is . . . things are never as
   good as you think they are and they're
   never as bad as you might think they are.
   They're somewhere in the middle.

Clinton had scheduled three one-on-one interviews
(radio, television, and print) that day to frame his State of
the Union Address (now less than a week away), including
an exchange with PBS *NewsHour* host Jim Lehrer. The State
of the Union wasn't the first question there either and he
denied any "improper relationship." He followed the same
script in interviews on National Public Radio and in the congressional newspaper *Roll Call*, so it was pretty clear as I went
on the air that night we were going to spend part of that
hour talking about the all-too-familiar "he said–she said." I
wasn't looking forward to it because all the talk becomes supposition. There were no witnesses. As I left for the Sunset
Boulevard studio to do the live section of the show, I looked
at my wife, Shawn, and made the observation, "I got a feeling this is a story that isn't going to go away for a while." It
ain't easy being a beacon of light.

We had a great panel to introduce the world to what will
become, if not the first sentence, certainly the first paragraph,

of the Clinton presidency. James Carville was the well-known spin doctor, who had been on the phone with the White House at least twenty times that day. Bob Woodward was assistant managing editor of the *Washington Post*. And Evan Thomas of *Newsweek* who heard ninety minutes of the taped conversations between Monica Lewinsky and Linda Tripp. The story, which first appeared in a Matt Drudge column on the Internet, said *Newsweek* was holding back publication. Thomas refused, as well he should have, to tell me how he got the tapes. And he said they were holding the story in order to check out facts. After that, I had other issues to understand.

> KING: Why does this push the pope in Havana and the Middle East peace talks to second and third in the news?
>
> WOODWARD: Well, because it's about sex and it's about the president. And there's this lingering question in the country and in the world about Clinton's credibility, and in fairness to him, there's been no witness who has come forward who is really credible who can say, I saw and participated in criminal activities. This seems to get a foot in the door on that issue. And people want a resolution of it.
>
> KING: So sex is still numero uno of interest?
>
> WOODWARD: With all deference to the pope, sex still triumphs.
>
> KING: . . . The end is like where?
>
> CARVILLE: You know, seventy-two hours, forty-eight minutes, and twenty-three

seconds. I don't know but we're all going to
know the truth.

When the show was over I thanked everyone and then
sat for a moment in the studio just thinking about the hour
and how it fit into the entire day. One thing was clear: The
Frenzy was going full throttle. I knew it because I kept thinking about the pope and the work he was trying to accom-
plish in Cuba and how the national conversation on relations
between these two countries was obliterated by the fact all
the network anchors packed their vests and were on the
quickest flight, if there is such a thing, from Havana back to
New York. I'm sure Fidel Castro was ticked at not being the
lead and not being photographed in a business suit with the
pope. Now that I think about it, I bet the pope was ticked
too. And if I ever interview him, that will be my second
question.

By the next day CNN, MSNBC, Fox, and the three networks were all running special reports with titles like "White
House in Crisis" or "Presidency in Crisis" or "White House
Under Fire." We hadn't gotten to the point where each day
starts getting numbered as in "Crisis Day 436," which began
with *Nightline* during the Iran Hostage Crisis in 1979, but I
knew that day was coming. After all, talk radio had spent
the past six years numbering the days in office of the Clinton administration, as if this was a miserable experience for
all of America, and I just knew the right-wing hosts were
smelling blood. This was a gift that had been handed to them
and I was certain the volume would be cranked all the way
up as they did the "I told you so" routine. But having been
in this business for a few years, I knew America was going
to take a wait-and-see approach to the story as it does through

every frenzy, despite the radio ranting, continuous TV coverage, and above-the-fold headlines. But it was The Topic. People couldn't get enough of it. That too is the stuff of a frenzy.

By the second night (okay, White House Crisis Day 2), *Larry King Live* was well into what would be more than one hundred full hours on the scandal. Among the guests was Mandy Grunwald, who had worked with Clinton on both White House campaigns.

> KING: As someone who knows the president and advised him a lot, what do you think he's like now?
>
> GRUNWALD: Probably the full range of emotions that he's known for. He is probably focused on his State of the Union Address and is blocking out everything else when he deals with that. He has an amazing ability to set these things into different boxes and deal with the work at hand. It's hard for the rest of us to understand how, with all of these charges going on, he could actually get any work done, but from all appearances he is.

See, another element of a frenzy is how days turn into seconds. The speed increases. The pundits were on all the shows saying Clinton should address the charges in the State of the Union Address, now six days away, he delivers to both houses of Congress because he will have the ears of the entire country. Of course, this was nuts because had Clinton said he was going to make a statement at 3:00 A.M. Sunday morning every television in America would have been tuned in, certainly more than would have watched the State of the Union Address.

The Topic at lunch the following day at Nate & Al's was Bill Clinton and January. It was decided the president has tough first months of the year: 1992 he had to deal with Gennifer Flowers on 60 Minutes, 1993 he delivered his first State of the Union Address and was trying to learn the job, the 1995 State of the Union ran almost an hour and a half, in 1997 he was delivering the State of the Union when the O.J. civil case verdict came in, and now he was dealing with Monica. We agreed this was the toughest January of all. And in the first week of "the crisis," we brought Gennifer Flowers into the studio.

> KING: How do you explain that such a bright
> person and a brilliant politician would get
> like this?
> FLOWERS: I don't think you want me to
> answer this and be honest.
> KING: Why? You know him. Why do bad
> things happen to good—
> FLOWERS: I'd think he was thinking with
> another head instead of this one.

I knew the floor technicians were cracking up as she said it because of the quick crouches taking place behind the cameras. In fact, I imagine there were howls erupting in homes across the world. It was a line I've heard for years and, while a sweeping generality, it is probably one of the truest statements made along with "lift to left field when hitting a ball out of Ebbets Field."

But anyone with the dream of running for president someday while watching these interviews that week had to be
doing a checklist of potential problem areas. And if they
weren't watching the show, well, they had better be doing
the checklist anyway. A frenzy can spread. I could see the
announcement twenty years later:

> My name is Zeb Biller and I'm running for president
> of the United States. In 1975 I got loaded while my
> wife was traveling, woke up with Zelda Gershenson.
> She is now a housewife in Otis, Indiana, and can be
> reached at 219-555-5555. In 1978 I met a girl in
> Chicago and we went out but I learned she was a he.
> You can reach Dave at . . .

It's a scary thought. If the country insists that in order
to be president there is a particular direction one's moral
compass must point, then all of these questions are relevant.
If not, then a candidate can say "that's none of your &%*
business." Or, we could keep doing things the way we do
them now, which is called "I don't know." And "I don't know"
works just fine. There was a time when Tom Johnson of CNN
asked me to write my thoughts about what questions are appropriate with regard to the private lives of candidates and
I said it can't be done. There are no rules, I told him. What
if we make a rule that you can't ask about a rumor? What if
that rumor appears on the front page of the *New York Times*
and is framed with the words "sources are saying"? What do
we do if other news groups don't follow the rule? Is this good?
The answer is it's moot.

And then there was the dress. It was blue. It was from
the Gap. And it had semen stains. As we went on the air

one evening I mentioned to the staff this story was starting to read like a bad novel and with this new element, the bad novel had just gotten worse. I talked with Dr. Henry Lee, with whom all of us first became acquainted during the O.J. trial, about plans to do a DNA test of the semen stain as a way of linking—or not linking—the president despite Clinton's claim he never had "sexual relations with that woman, Ms. Lewinsky." Lee said if a match isn't made, the president is off the hook. We were coming out of the second commercial break of the show, and I realized the entire country was focused on presidential semen and a dress and an intern. I took the cue from the floor director and turned to Evan Thomas of *Newsweek*.

> KING: Did you ever think we would be on international television talking about this subject?
> THOMAS: No, I mean this is beyond belief but here we are talking about it.
> KING: Why did we get to this?
> THOMAS: Well, for a lot of reasons: a very aggressive prosecutor, an aggressive media, but also a president of the United States who apparently got himself into this fix.

The ratings were good for these shows. It was Jackie Gleason who had told me so many years earlier in Miami that he could win the Saturday night time slot by just doing sex. "Give me a good-looking couple," he said, "and I can get better ratings. The thing is, going the sex route takes absolutely no ingenuity at all." We weren't going the sex route because there were greater issues: credibility with Congress,

191

effectiveness with world leaders, and the state of the national soul. And that took ingenuity. But we talked about sex in every show. And I will tell you I was uncomfortable talking about it the first few times but, within a month of the story first being heard, talking about oral sex became the same as talking about Iraq.

The president didn't allude to his problems during the State of the Union Address but ratings were better than for previous speeches. People tuned in to listen for the words. See, that's another definition of frenzy: You listen and watch and read something you normally wouldn't, just on the chance of getting one more nugget. In her first public statement Hillary Clinton told Matt Lauer on NBC there was "a vast right-wing conspiracy" fueling the charges against the president. I was more than aware when things didn't go the way the White House hoped or expected that they would say the Haters were at work again. You're either with me or against me and if you're not with me then you must be a Hater. So this latest remark was simply a variation on a theme. I thought of a conversation I'd had on the air with Texas Republican Dick Armey during the debate about the Contract With America, and his view of the Clinton White House on bad days. "Jimmy Carter said 'I don't know what's wrong with my presidency. I guess it's because the American people are filled with malaise.' Clinton says 'I don't know what's wrong with my presidency,'" Armey told me. " 'It's because the American people are full of malice.' " But there were also occasions, such as health care, where many in Congress as well as industry experts thought the Clinton White House just had a bad policy.

The conspiracy wasn't made up of a bunch of guys sitting around a shack in Montana with a copy of the Bill of

Rights and wearing camouflage. For one, those folks aren't going to like the Republican way of doing things either. For another, they aren't going to let Mrs. Clinton know they exist, so if she has just blown their cover on national television the vast right-wing conspiracy is going to have to look for another job. So I wasn't buying the idea that the president's problems were the work of the Haters quietly talking to each other. In this case, I figured it was the result of his own poor judgment.

Six weeks into the story we decided to bring on the great thinkers of the country to analyze the current situation and offer a perspective, quite possibly, that had yet to be considered. Political pundits, who have day jobs as comedians, John Stewart and Al Franken, appeared together:

> KING: Why is this like a runaway freight train?
> STEWART: Because in conversational rock,
> scissors, paper, oral sex beats almost
> everything. You can go on stage and talk
> about racism and religion and things but
> boy, oral sex, people love to talk about, and
> presidential oral sex? That's just, there's
> nothing better.
> KING: Al, your thoughts on the humor in this?
> FRANKEN: I'm troubled. And we don't know.
> Nothing has been—
> KING: All of it is conjecture.
> FRANKEN: Right. And CNN, I've been
> watching a lot of you and Jeff Greenfield
> did that show on media frenzy.
> KING: Right.

> FRANKEN: —and talked a lot about get it first
> or get it right. So a lot of this is about leaks
> that aren't proven. But there have been a
> number of news organizations that have not
> rushed to judgment. I'd like to salute them.
> KING: Go ahead.
> FRANKEN: *Sailing Magazine. American Grocer
> Monthly.*

People still tell me that show made more sense than anything else on television that evening. And Franken was right.
I read *American Grocer Monthly* all the time and they still
haven't gone out on a limb with the story.

I was on *Today* talking to Matt Lauer about a book I'd
written and after doing the required thirty seconds of the interview on the book, we spent the remaining three minutes
talking about Monica. The topic was how everyone wanted
a chance to have the first interview with her.

"Look, if I had God in the green room and Monica in
the green room and both said this was the only time they
had in their schedules for me to ask a few questions, I'd look
at God and ask if we could find another time to talk." It
wasn't shtick. I was serious.

That night I had a book party at Morton's restaurant in
Washington, D.C. It was the old Duke Zeibert's location and
even though the interior and the menu were new, in my head
I could still see the old booths and Duke standing at the
podium. He had died a few years earlier and as I went in for
the party I thought about the great old guy and the jokes he
would be telling right now. Tim Russert was the host of the
party and Senator John Warner, Bill Safire, Greta Van Susteren, and Wolf Blitzer of CNN were there along with about

150 other guests. It was my wife, Shawn, who pulled me aside and said, "Look who's standing over there." I followed her finger into the crowd and saw Monica Lewinsky.

Producers at the television show had invited her attorney, William Ginsburg, to the party and in doing so added, "and bring Monica if she'd like to attend." Nobody thought any more about it until she appeared. We had a good conversation, if you can have a good conversation with a hundred people listening in.

"I just needed to get out," she said, "it's been crazy." She was right. More people were asking her to sign copies of my book than me. She didn't. I did.

I told her she would get through this and that her father and stepmother are good friends of mine, and when she is able to talk publicly, *Larry King Live* would be the show to do. While she and I were talking, John Warner became aware of who was in the room with him and left. He didn't want to be photographed because the picture could wind up with a future opponent, or if this issue went to the Senate, he could be charged with being partial. Word had spread quickly and soon all the cameras were lined up on Connecticut Avenue staking out the restaurant, staking out the underground parking lot, staking out every entrance to the building. Reporters were trying to talk their way into the party saying they had an invitation. This was the moment I understood the phrase "feeding frenzy." Though we were in a great steakhouse, it turned into a tank of piranhas and Monica was the source of food.

Monica and Ginsburg had dinner at Morton's that night. When I left to go to work, the camera crews were still staked out on the street and producers were asking me what she talked about, how's her mood, did she wear a blue dress, and every other possible insane question. I understood they were doing their job and I'd have watched their reports that night or the next morning but to paraphrase Ernest Hollings: Like laws, news just ain't pretty to watch being made. Morton's managers say that book party was the best night they've had to date and I can certainly understand why. The place was packed and any available table was taken by someone wearing a media credential. A lot of newsrooms bought dinner at Morton's that night and I hope it cost them big-time because the fact I had written a book wasn't mentioned in any of the stories about the Monica Watch.

Bill Clinton was subpoenaed August 17 and spent more than four hours answering questions from Ken Starr. As he did, the president's "senior advisors," as they were called, put the word out that Mr. Clinton would admit to having an improper relationship with Monica Lewinsky. When I heard this, the first thought was about Newt Gingrich. More back flips. Maybe even a high-five. Those who disliked Clinton had been given one more gift, they now had a president who had an eighteen-month affair with an intern, lied about it to the country for seven months, and now was probably going to have to face the music in front of a national television audience. House Republicans were pushing congressional hearings before the House Judiciary Committee using the mantra that lying about the affair was a high crime or misdemeanor.

It wasn't. It was sex. Lying about sex has taken place since Adam, if he had anyone else to talk to other than Eve. It wasn't national security. It wasn't compromising state secrets. Yet House Republicans like Bob Barr and Dan Burton, both of whom I like and enjoy interviewing, continued to insist it was lying, which it was, and he should be impeached, which was ridiculous. This was the line of demarcation. And it had become its own frenzy. Despite the fact Americans didn't approve of the president's behavior, most viewed lying about sex as a shallow reason to throw him out of office. Now, if the economy was tanking, the story would have been different.

That night the White House announced that the president would address the country. I went on the set that night thinking about the phrase "must give the speech of his life," which I have heard for every president during key moments when opinions needed to be swayed or a consensus made stronger. I knew if there ever was a moment for Bill Clinton to give the speech of his life, it was now. The atmosphere was, to say the least, charged. In studio with me was Congressman Bob Barr of Georgia, who was leading the Republican effort to hold impeachment hearings.

> KING: Do you feel like you're kicking a
> downed person if you continue with the
> impeachment tries?
> BARR: The fact of the matter is that all the
> talk is going around here as if this were the
> end of the matter and we have a president
> that we need to rally behind and so forth,
> as if there's been a death in the family or
> some crisis beyond his control. This is a
> situation of his own making.
> KING: Yeah but why not forgive him and rally
> around him in the good ethic of what
> makes America, the great Judeo-Christian
> ethic, forgive, let's go on?

> BARR: Well, what we've inherited and what
> we have an obligation to uphold is the rule
> of law and accountability in America.

Also with me was James Carville who had talked with Clinton at the White House just a few minutes earlier, saying the president appeared focused and was making last-minute changes to his address. If a talk show is supposed to bring a listener or a viewer as close as possible to a story, we were doing just that. And I was proud of the entire effort. We were moving toward an unknown—what would the president say and how would it be received—and it made the evening all the more exciting. Of course, Carville can do that on his own.

> CARVILLE: History has taught us that time
> and time and time again, brilliant, powerful
> leaders have made errors in judgment when
> it comes to people of the opposite sex,
> because it's harder the first time it happens.
> What has happened here that I find so
> disturbing is that we are trying to
> criminalize this stuff, which is absolutely
> ludicrous. And it would take a hundred
> psychiatrists a hundred years to explain why
> do people with so much to lose—
> KING: No president ever had this happen to
> him—
> CARVILLE: No—
> KING: Had his sexual life under trial?
> CARVILLE: Had his sex life on trial.

During the segment, Carville didn't ask any questions as to how the Orioles might make up some key games, which was proof enough that even he was worried about how the evening was going to turn out.

Bob Woodward was with me in the studio and offered one more piece of advice about how the speech would be received. He said the word at the White House had always been to look into the eyes of Leon Panetta to gauge how well Clinton does. The former chief of staff was with us by satellite from Monterey. The pressure was now turned up one more notch.

And then Bill Clinton came on. He spoke four and a half minutes, spent most of it going after Ken Starr and, from my take, bombed.

I went to James Carville, who said the president apologized and accepted responsibility. But his words weren't ringing true with me. He was spinning. So I turned to Bob Barr.

> BARR: All the president said was "leave me alone. I'm not going to tell you what really happened. I'm not going to—"
> KING: He said he had an improper relationship. You didn't want to know all the details, did you? Did you want to know every sex act?
> BARR: I don't really care about the improper relationship at all. What I care about is obstruction of justice, tampering with witnesses, subornation of perjury, possible destruction of evidence.

199

Barr wasn't going to give an inch. We had a word in Brooklyn when someone was set in their way: grangles. It's the fingernails-on-the-chalkboard thing. Bob Barr was giving me grangles. He never moved off his position. He was a bright guy but you could sit there all day and talk and he would be using the same line after ten hours that he used the first thirty seconds. He was spinning too. So I went to Leon Panetta and looked in his eyes.

> KING: What did you think, Leon?
> PANETTA: . . . The president of the United
> States acknowledged an illicit relationship
> in the White House, and he has apologized
> not only to his wife and his daughter but to
> the United States of America. You know,
> this isn't the end but it's certainly the
> beginning of the end.

He was spinning as well. I didn't have a White House aide to ask about the read in Panetta's eyes but I think we were all feeling let down. Now, it can be argued we *should* be disappointed after all the buildup because great expectations don't always deliver. I wasn't subscribing to that logic one iota. Bill Clinton said "I misled people" but, despite what Panetta and Carville were saying, he never used the words "I'm sorry."

Bob Shrum watched it from Sun Valley, Utah, where he was winding up a vacation. He had been in conversations with Clinton's pollster, Mark Penn, at the White House about this very moment and what words the president might use to be politically, legally, and personally accurate all at the same time. With an assurance that Mark would be at the other end of a fax machine, he sent a rough draft for a possible speech. It was never given. It used the words "I apologize." I talked to him about it off the air a year later.

> I figured he was under a lot of pressure all day long
> and the biggest mistake was to have given the speech
> the same day. He needed to wait twenty-four hours
> and get rid of the anger.

Bill Clinton left the White House the next day with Hillary and Chelsea to spend a week on Cape Cod trying to put his family back together again. The picture of them walking to *Marine One* on the South Lawn was poignant. I watched it live on TV and was overcome with the feeling that I shouldn't be looking at this private moment. And, of course, I stayed with the scene until the helicopter lifted off. Clinton was back within forty-eight hours, though. The United States had launched cruise missiles into Sudan and Afghanistan knocking out a chemical weapons factory and a training facility for terrorist Osama bin Laden. Clinton went back on the air explaining the reasons for the action and later said he had been working on the final details of the plan to attack before he testified in front of Ken Starr. The critics started up saying this was the theme of the movie *Wag the Dog,* where a president invents a conflict to improve poll numbers, suggesting Clinton wanted to get the public attention off his character. I shook my head while listening to talk radio hosts go rabid one more time. Even if you were, to use the White House term for the opposition, a Hater, you had to understand Bill Clinton was still president. Had he done nothing, they would have said "where was he?" It was lose-lose. And this was the moment I realized whenever and wherever this story comes to an end, there will be no winners.

Ken Starr sent the House 445 pages detailing every meeting President Clinton had with Monica Lewinsky and what exactly happened during each meeting. The House decided to release the report less than twenty-four hours after receiving it, saying if they didn't, the White House would put its spin team to work and make the report favorable to the president. It showed up on the Internet, in newspapers, in magazines, and it was a best-seller for a few weeks in bookstores. This was a time when I found myself asking the question, "If the American people were asked, 'Do you want to spend $50 million on this?' most would answer no thanks." There had been numerous convictions, including the governor of Arkansas and the president's good friend, former justice official Webster Hubbel. And the question was raised as to whether or not a sitting president can be indicted after leaving office. Today, we're still debating that one. But in the minds of my lunch friends and many people across America, it was about sex.

Of course, it depends on how you define sex. Just when I was telling everyone at lunch this whole thing couldn't get more wacko, we started reading and hearing Bill Clinton say oral sex wasn't sex. He wasn't putting anyone on; he believed it. This was fantastic. It was Maureen Dowd who made the astute observation if it wasn't sex, then it wouldn't have the word "sex" attached. See, these are the great issues we were facing as the millennium came to an end. I wish I had Bill Clinton's definition when I was a teenager in Brooklyn because we all thought oral sex, while a rarity, was sex.

And then came election day. Minnesota voted in a former professional wrestler to be its next governor. Democrats won five seats in the House. A few days later, Newt Gingrich quit. Had you told me when the year began that the president would have an affair with an intern and by year's end Newt Gingrich would be the one without a job, I'd have politely replied, "That's crazy."

The television show stayed with every nuance in the drive toward an impeachment vote in the House Judiciary Committee. Ross Perot came on and announced he would lead a march on Washington to call for Clinton's resignation, saying the president had lost the ability to lead. Book agent Lucianne Goldberg talked about her role in having Linda Tripp tape Monica Lewinsky and the major players on the Judiciary Committee appeared to discuss the day's events. Though the subject stayed the same, I was learning something new every night. Roseanne came on to push her daytime talk show and announce she would pay a million dollars for the first on-camera sit-down with Monica Lewinsky. Monica had signed a seven-figure book deal and the word was out Barbara Walters would have the first interview. I had been making phone calls to Bernard Lewinsky and Monica's stepmother throughout the year and had called Monica to wish her a happy birthday and to keep us in mind when she was ready to talk. Getting a guest could no longer be done in one letter or one phone call. It involved making a strong case as to what this show could do. And in my case, it meant I wasn't going to pay Monica one dime because CNN, rightly so, doesn't operate that way. But Roseanne had a different take about Barbara Walters's potential exclusive:

> They are going to interview her in February. I know
> that means sweeps and sweeps means ratings and

ratings—each point of ratings is $6 million at least.

So the news is for sale and the news is about money.

Also on the panel that night was First Amendment lawyer Floyd Abrams and *Washington Post* media critic Howard Kurtz. We took a call from Santa Clara, California, about the yet-to-be-announced Monica interview.

> CALLER: Why do we have to listen to this again?
>
> ROSEANNE: I don't think we've even heard the beginning.
>
> ABRAMS: I think the public has had it. The caller speaks for America.
>
> KURTZ: You know, you don't need the whole country to watch. All you need is a significant enough part of the audience to keep cable shows afloat and to keep Barbara Walters happy. And I think you'll get those kind of numbers. If the public didn't care, we'd be sitting here talking about Iraq.

At about the time the House Judiciary Committee voted to send all four articles of impeachment to the full House, there *was* talk about Iraq. A lot of talk. And then it went to the next step. Saddam Hussein had forbid U.N. weapons inspectors admittance to palaces to search for chemical and biological weapons. When he had done the same thing a month earlier, the United States had planes in the air going after Iraqi military targets but U.N. Secretary General Kofi Annan stepped in and convinced Hussein to rethink his inspection ban. He did and the planes returned. When inspectors were refused entrance again, Operation Desert Fox began over Baghdad with 210 aircraft and more than 300 cruise missiles. The House postponed the impeachment debate for a day and it now appeared there would be a vote over the weekend.

The bombing of Iraq continued into a second night and I had the Iraqi ambassador to the United Nations, Nizar Hamdoon, in our New York studio. In Baghdad with bombs dropping in the background we had CNN's Christiane Amanpour. Ambassador Hamdoon was furious with the bombing of his country and said an arrangement could be worked out any time Bill Clinton wanted to negotiate. We went to a commercial break as another explosion hit behind Christiane. I looked at Hamdoon and thought to myself, I wonder what it is he *can't* tell me? That's when he started talking.

"Larry?"

"Yes, Mr. Ambassador."

"When are you coming to New York?"

"I have no idea, Mr. Ambassador. Especially with all that is going on."

"Well, call me when you are making a trip here and we can have lunch." He was smiling.

I looked at my countdown clock and saw we only had a few seconds before we came back live. But I'm thinking, this guy has just invited me to lunch and my country is dropping cruise missiles all over his country and we have twenty-two ships on site in the Gulf with aircraft. I quickly thanked him and said when I get a better fix on my schedule I'll certainly be in touch. And as I'm counted out of the commercial break my mind isn't on what I'm going to say but, rather, on how, in only a few minutes, the world has become completely crazy. Or was it always like this?

Two days later I'm at home in California doing a few miles on the treadmill, clicker in hand, newspaper on the tray, and watching CNN. The impeachment vote is under-way in the House and as I'm coming up on the three-quarter-mile mark, a crawl comes across the screen saying Speaker-designate Bob Livingston was resigning because he had an affair during his thirty-three-year marriage. It was the result of Larry Flynt's earlier offer of a million dollars for in-formation on the sexual history of members of Congress. Yeah, the treadmill stopped. We were going to work again that night and I figured, the way things were moving, we would probably be working nonstop for the rest of the year.

I picked up the phone and dialed the White House. Wendy had suggested I call the president and suggest he come on and talk about what the day has been like. I gave the president's personal secretary, Betty Currie, the message and went back to the impeachment vote until the Jets-Buffalo game came on.

The house voted to impeach Bill Clinton on two of the four counts. This meant it was now in the hands of the Sen-ate. Clinton appeared at the White House with congressional Democrats and cabinet members to vow he would fight to complete his term. I knew this was history. Everyone watch-ing television or listening on the radio that moment knew the same thing.

Two hours later Clinton was back on camera to announce the bombing of Iraq would end after four nights of air strikes from U.S. and British forces. I watched the statement and clicked to the Redskins–Tampa Bay game underway at Jack Kent Cooke Stadium. It was the third quarter and the Skins were losing. That's when the phone rang. It was my private line. Nobody had that number other than Shawn and Wendy. I picked it up.

A man's voice came on the phone sounding official. "Please hold for the president," he said.

I hit the volume control on the clicker. And while I'm doing this I'm thinking, "the president of what?" The volume wasn't changing. The clicker needed a battery, which meant I was going to buy a new clicker because I have yet to figure out how to put in batteries.

The voice came back on. "Mr. King, the president is going to the private residence so it will be just another moment or so." Now I knew what was going on. But it was tough to hear because I couldn't lower the TV volume. I walked toward the back of the room as far as the phone cord would let me go.

"Hey, Larry. How you doing?"

I knew the voice right away. "How are you, Mr. President?"

There was a pause. "Is that the Redskins game?"

"Yes sir, it sure is." The crowd was really getting loud as happens at Redskins games. The phone cord wouldn't stretch any further. What's worse, the mute button didn't work either.

"Who's winning?"

"Well, Mr. President, Tampa Bay is ahead 16–7 but the Skins are driving."

"Yeah? Who won the Jets game? I've been distracted all day."

I'm thinking here. This is the president of the United States and he's asking me football scores. This is the president of the United States and he has just been impeached.

207

This is the president of the United States and no less than ten minutes ago I watched him on TV saying this country is no longer going to bomb Iraq halfway around the world. I had read about his ability to compartmentalize things but not until now did I understand what it meant.

"Jets won it. They get the division title. Took the Bills 17–10." I was going to tell him about the seventy-one-yard Vinnie Testaverde touchdown pass to Dedric Ward, but decided, instead, to take advantage of this opportunity. "Mr. President," I said, "we've known each other a long time and this has been a weird day in America."

Clinton started talking about how sorry he was to see Livingston resign and he didn't think that was the correct way to go and he should have stayed in and fought. And he talked about how he admired Republican congressman Peter King, who went against his party and voted not to impeach.

I asked him to appear and he thanked me for the offer. And he thanked me for doing a fair show.

"I'll give you two, three hours. It would be good for you to do and you're good at it," I added. Clinton stayed noncommittal.

"How is Shawn doing with a baby on the way?"

"Fine. We are expecting him in March," I said.

"Well, Hillary and I are praying he looks like your wife."

The president wasn't the first one to make that observation. We said goodbye and I walked toward the TV to hang up the phone. The crowd was going crazy because the Skins had just scored on a fifteen-yard Stephen Alexander run. Nobody at Jack Kent Cooke Stadium was thinking about what had happened in the past six hours. I think everyone in America that day was ready for a football game.

Clinton consultant Bob Shrum's proposed August 17, 1998, speech for Clinton that wasn't given:

> No one who is not in my position can understand fully the remorse I feel today. Since I was very young, I've had a profound reverence for this office I hold. I've been honored that you, the people, have entrusted it to me. I am proud of what we have accomplished together.
>
> But in this case, I have fallen short of what you should expect from a president. I have failed my own religious faith and values. I have let too many people down. I take full responsibility for my actions, for hurting my wife and daughter, for hurting Monica Lewinsky, for hurting friends and staff, and for hurting the country I love. None of this should have happened.
>
> I never should have had any sexual contact with Monica Lewinsky. But I did. I should have acknowledged that I was wrong months ago. But I didn't. I thought I was shielding my family but I know that in the end, for Hillary and Chelsea, delay has only brought more pain. Their forgiveness and love, expressed so often as we sat alone together this weekend, means far more than I can ever say.
>
> What I did was wrong—and there was no excuse for it. I do want to assure you, as I told the grand jury under oath, that I did nothing to obstruct this investigation.
>
> Finally, I also want to apologize to all of you, my fellow citizens. I hope you can find it in your heart to accept that apology. I pledge to you that I will make

every effort of mind and spirit to earn your confidence again, to be worthy of this office, and to finish the work in which we have made such remarkable progress for the past six years.

Clinton's August 17, 1998, speech from the Oval Office:

This afternoon, from this chair, I testified before the Office of Independent Counsel and the grand jury. I answered their questions truthfully, including questions about my private life, questions no American citizens would ever want to answer.

Still, I must take complete responsibility for all my actions, both public and private. And that is why I am speaking to you tonight. As you know, in a deposition in January, I was asked questions about my relationship with Monica Lewinsky. While my answers were legally accurate, I did not volunteer information. Indeed, I did have a relationship with Miss Lewinsky that was not appropriate. In fact, it was wrong. It constituted a critical lapse in judgment and a personal failure on my part for which I am solely and completely responsible.

But I told the grand jury today and I say to you now that at no time did I ask anyone to lie, to hide or destroy evidence, or to take any other unlawful action.

I know that my public comments and my silence about this matter gave a false impression. I misled people, including even my wife. I deeply regret that.

I can only tell you that I was motivated by many factors. First, by a desire to protect myself from the embarrassment of my own conduct.

I was also very concerned about protecting my family. The fact that these questions were being asked in a politically inspired lawsuit, which has since been dismissed, was a consideration too. In addition I had real and serious concerns about an independent counsel investigation that began with private business dealings twenty years ago, dealings I might add about which an independent federal agency found no evidence of any wrongdoing by me or my wife over two years ago.

The independent counsel investigation moved on to my staff and friends, then into my private life. And now the investigation itself is under investigation.

This has gone on too long, cost too much, and hurt too many innocent people.

Now, this matter is between me, the two people I love most—my wife and our daughter—and our God. I must put it right and I am prepared to do whatever it takes to do so.

Nothing is more important to me personally. But it is private and I intend to reclaim my family life for my family. It's nobody's business but ours. Even presidents have private lives. It is time to stop the pursuit of personal destruction and the prying into private lives and get on with our national life.

Our country has been distracted by this matter for too long and I take my responsibility for my part in all of this. That is all I can do. Now it is time, in fact it is past time, to move on. We have important work to do—real opportunities to seize, real problems to solve, real security matters to face.

And so tonight, I ask you to turn away from the spectacle of the past seven months, to repair the fabric of our national discourse, and to return our attention to all of the challenges and all of the promise of the next American century.

CHAPTER EIGHT

Whatever

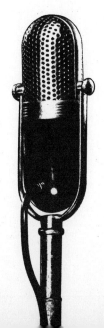

January 1999. There was a crisis for Bill Clinton but, compared to other Januarys, this one wasn't much of a concern, if an impeachment trial in the United States Senate could ever be in that category. I'd spent the holidays in Los Angeles, with a new TV clicker, and nobody mentioned impeachment. There was some talk about Chief Justice William Rehnquist's modified black robe with the stripes on each sleeve and how he looked like a member of the New York Rangers, but zero on throwing the president out of office.

In Washington, D.C., though, impeachment was still The Topic. And there was something else: Bill Clinton had a State of the Union Address to deliver. People weren't talking about whether he might go for ninety minutes, as was the usual angst when Clinton and State of the Union were used in the same sentence. Instead, it was whether he should give the speech at all.

The address was to be delivered on Capitol Hill to both houses of Congress. For Bill Clinton, one house had just impeached him and the other was holding a trial that could result in his being removed from office. This wasn't exactly an audience ready for applause, if you get my drift. So the issue became, should he wait until a decision is made in the Senate before giving the State of the Union? That's how I explained it to Herb Cohen at lunch one day.

"So what's the problem?" he asked.

"There is concern about whether he should mention a pending impeachment when he talks to both houses or if he should wait until the trial is over," I said.

"Larry, is he going to give a State of the Union Address if he gets thrown out?"

"Of course not."

"So I come back to the initial question. What's the problem?" Herb was looking at me the way he used to when we were kids in front of Sid's Pants on 83rd Street. He was a Yankee fan, I was a Dodger fan, and, as a result, there were only two arguments for any issue.

"Should Clinton say anything about the situation if he gives the State of the Union Address as scheduled while the trial is going on?" I asked.

"No."

I couldn't let it drop right there, so I started in. "Look, the guy is standing in a charged atmosphere. There are strong opponents in the audience and this is a chance to face them and say I'm doing the business of the people or whatever it is he always says about working for America."

"No."

"It will take the edge off if he faces it right away," I said, "because the public will see this isn't a distraction whatsoever."

Herb looked at me. "I'm going to have the salad with tuna." We didn't talk about the State of the Union for the rest of the day.

But it was the topic at an event that evening in Washington attended by the Clintons and the Gores. Shawn and I were invited, and as soon as we arrived, the issue began. Okay, I brought it up. We said hello to Ann Lewis, who had been a deputy campaign manager in the 1996 Clinton–Gore campaign and now worked at the White House. Lewis was one of the many faces we had seen on television, including my show, defending the president over the past year. She was with her husband, Mike Sponder.

"If I were advising him," I said, "I'd say refer to the impeachment issue. Everyone will be waiting for him to do it."

Sponder was having none of it. At first he did that Washington thing in which you listen politely while something insane is said, then smile and say, "That's an interesting idea." In Brooklyn, I would have heard "What? Are you crazy?" at least three times by now. I pressed on.

"Here's what I'd say," I went on. " 'You know it's weird standing here where half this place has impeached me and the other half is judging me, but you know what? I've got a country to run.' That would get the issue behind and show there are more important things to do."

Sponder smiled. He was going to do it again, I thought to myself.

"Look, Mike," I said, "he's got the audience watching and I'll bet zero of them are waiting to hear what he thinks of gold bullion. They are tuned in to get some kind of nuance."

Ann Lewis was watching this and enjoying it. I've seen

her eat opponents for lunch in debates. And I think it's in the DNA because her brother is Massachusetts congressman Barney Frank, who is one of the best debaters I've seen. Sponder smiled again.

"Larry," he said, "you do what you do very well but your skill is not politics."

He had me and he did it in one sentence. Obviously, the ability to debate isn't in the DNA.

I caught Clinton's eye and he waved for us to come over. "Larry, how you doing?" He smiled. He took Shawn's hand and asked how she was feeling. The guy was facing a Senate trial and you'd have never caught, as I had just argued, any nuance of concern. Clinton said he had seen me on the Reverend Robert Schuller's Sunday show and that he enjoyed the segment.

"March, right?" he asked Shawn. He remembered. That's when Chance was going to be born. Less than seven weeks from now.

He looked at me. "And you're sixty-five, right?"

"That's right, Mr. President," I said.

"And you had heart surgery. But the fact you had the surgery and you are sixty-five and you're in good shape and you haven't had cancer, heck you're going to make it to eighty-three, maybe longer." He had all these statistics. I run a cardiac foundation and I didn't know this stuff.

"You know, being a father at your age has got to be just great. Look at George Mitchell over there," he said nodding toward the former Senate majority leader, who was now leading efforts to find peace in Northern Ireland, "you ought to talk to him. And you ought to talk to Norman Lear. I bet it's just wonderful. I'd like to be a father at that age." He wasn't just making conversation. He meant it.

Clinton started talking to some other people, so I picked up a menu from a nearby table to see what was going to be served. And that was the moment Vice President and Tipper Gore came by. "Larry, you're my good-luck charm," he said, referring to the NAFTA debate from six years earlier. We talked about his upcoming presidential campaign.

"If I'm the good-luck charm, then come on the show and announce," I urged.

Nothing doing. Gore said he was going to announce from his hometown. That wasn't the answer I wanted but, in these days of satellites where one can talk across countries, it was good to see a candidate choose the real world over the television studio. Of course, when you think about it, today the television studio *is* the real world.

"And I still remember that show in Nashville," Gore said smiling. We had been at Vanderbilt University a year earlier and did a live show at Kirkland Hall where the vice president attended a conference on family involvement in a child's education. Gore had talked about his days there as a law student and Tipper reflected on her master's program in psychology at Vanderbilt. Gore had gone long on his last answer and I had to jump in, thank them, and promote the next show, which was going to be with the scientist involved in the cloning of Dolly, a sheep in Scotland. And in my headset I had a producer saying "Get out, get out" while a floor director in front of me was doing frantic hand signals. When Gore took a breath, I jumped in and said, "We're out of time folks, thank you, Mr. Vice President and Mrs. Gore, and tomorrow night we talk to the guy who did the sheep. Good night from Nashville." It took three seconds. I got out right on time.

Gore was bent over, he was laughing so hard. And then I heard it in my earpiece.

"The guy who did the sheep?"

Here's what my job is like: I spend an hour interviewing the vice president and now the whole thing is remembered by a three-second miscue. While Gore was still cracking up next to me in Nashville, I sat there thinking either we were going to have great ratings in another twenty-four hours or this was going to become part of the CNN Christmas blooper tape. It was the latter.

So we went through the story one more time. As this is going on, I'm still looking at the menu and I see the entrée is Chilean sea bass. I looked up at Gore and said to myself, "Why not?"

"Does Chilean sea bass really come from Chile?" I asked.

Gore thought for one second and answered, "Larry, how the hell do I know?"

"If you are going to be president, you are going to have to be more definitive," I shot back.

Gore thought for another second. "No," he said loudly. People turned their heads to see what had upset the vice president. "If it doesn't come from Chile then I'm going to investigate because the public is being fooled. Now hear me clearly, this could become a standard of my campaign!" I wanted to applaud.

Bill Clinton is listening to all of this. He looks at me and says, "Who cares?" I could tell the rest of the second term was going to be coasting. And I knew one other thing: The State of the Union Address would be delivered as scheduled without any reference to impeachment. I couldn't imagine any fool thinking otherwise.

*   *   *

The next morning I had a phone call with George W. Bush, the Texas governor, the son of the former president, former part-owner of the Texas Rangers, and the hands-down front-runner to win the Republican nomination to be president of the United States. And for the first minute we talked about the campaign. He told me there were a few issues that had to be addressed before any formal announcement for a run was going to be made. One was the business of Texas. A second was what this campaign was going to do to his family.

"It's different from being a governor, that's for sure," I said. "And you are going to have Secret Service around you, which, from what little I know, can get to you after a while."

Bush told me the rigors of a campaign was a big issue, and while he was up to it physically, he wanted to make sure his wife and children were prepared for what they were going to have to face. The conversation made me wonder why anyone would want to do this. It just had to be easier when George Washington campaigned. He only had to face John Adams, invent a cabinet to serve with him, design the executive branch of government, and maintain neutrality in the war between Great Britain and France. Piece of cake.

The rest of the conversation was about baseball. While running the Texas Rangers, Bush was the only owner to vote against the wild card team in baseball playoffs. He was against the designated hitter rule. (The DH rule is used in the American League but not in the National League and it's a perennial argument. Personally, I like seeing the differences between the leagues and the DH rule makes it possible.) He was a purist, which was why he was in the minority. Bush talked about the many times the Rangers came close to getting in the World Series. "We need another pitcher and we'll make it to the big show in October." For George W., however, there was a bigger show pending and it was more than a year away. He sounded as though the pitchers were already on board for that one.

There was a more immediate campaign going on. In the Senate, House managers were still trying to convince sixty-seven senators (two-thirds majority) that Bill Clinton deserved to be thrown out of office. It wasn't going to happen because the fifty-five Republicans needed a dozen of the forty-five Democrats to vote for impeachment. And that math was based on the idea all the Republicans would vote the party line. So the result was known. When people were asked if there should be a trial, most said no. Did they think Clinton was honest and had integrity? No. But when the same people were asked if they liked the job President Clinton was doing, most said yes. This was a scene right out of *Fiddler on the Roof* where Tevye, the dairyman, is pressed by people in his village about the fact his daughter wants to marry a guy who isn't Jewish. How could he let this happen, they ask? Tevye answers, "I like him." I put the question to Senator Robert Byrd (D-WVa) one night:

> KING: Does the mood of the American public—the opinions—should that affect this trial?
> BYRD: It absolutely does and I don't think any president will ever be removed from office when the economy is at record highs.
> KING: And he's popular?
> BYRD: . . . Any president that's going to get the blame if the economy goes bad, he's going to get credited if it's good. So I came to the

conclusion, quite a while ago, that this
president would not be removed.

Something else was happening. Senators had been sworn
in by Chief Justice Rehnquist to be impartial jurors. And yet
every day we were getting the daily counts as to how badly
the pro-impeachment side was going to lose, so, somewhere,
someone was forming an opinion about the case. In fact,
many of them would sit all day listening to the arguments
and then come on the show in the evening to talk about
what they had heard and why they were going to vote a particular way.

There was a moment in early February, however, when I
thought my head was going to explode if I heard someone
in a pinstripe suit talk for the 2,859th time about "working
in the spirit of bipartisanship." It was the result of having listened for almost a year to the pinstripes in the House use
the same word to the point it actually became meaningless.
I was sitting with the clicker watching senators hold yet another news conference about being "bipartisan." My eyes
started to roll into my head. So I clicked to the Spanish-
speaking soccer game, which brought them back into focus.
I think it was the same game I had watched before but it always made sense despite the fact I still didn't understand soccer and I certainly didn't know Spanish. Those words,
whatever they were, at least had meaning.

This was happening to a lot of words on Capitol Hill.
"Send a message" makes my eyes roll back. Everyone sends
a message but, let me tell you, I don't think anyone receives
it. Just think if we could stop, for a moment, all the mes-
sages being sent. It would be busier than air traffic control
at JFK Airport. And while a lot would be taking off, noth-

ing would be landing. Another word is "rededicate," as in "it's time to rededicate ourselves to" . . . blah blah blah. It's nothing other than code for "we haven't been paying attention." And then, of course, if we must go around all the time and "rededicate" ourselves to some goal, well, does this mean it isn't enough to simply dedicate yourself to something in the first place?

All of this came to a head that afternoon after the soccer game was over. A spectator sitting in the public gallery of the Senate stood up as a vote was being taken and yelled, "God almighty, take the vote. Get it over with!"

This was the mother lode of defining moments. Everyone in the Senate that day had been talking about "the will of the American people" (another meaningless phrase), but the guy who was being thrown out of the gallery and arrested was the only one actually expressing it. Every news operation reported it. Suddenly, there was a hero coming out of this. I figured we were going to see him in a ticker tape parade, he might even be a guest on the show that night (he was still in jail when we went on the air), and depending on how things went in the Senate, maybe Clinton would recognize him in the next State of the Union Address.

Despite the fact it sounds like a contradiction in terms, the Senate moved quickly through the impeachment trial. And, of course, predictions were being made every day as to what the outcome was going to be or what the vote tally was going to be or, for those who were really good at this, what senators would defect to the other side. It was the same thing we see every Sunday during an NFL pregame show when pundits tell us what the score will be and why. As that vote drew closer, I asked columnist P. J. O'Rourke and Senator Christopher Bond (R-Mo.) to predict the outcome:

KING: What do you think is going to happen?

O'ROURKE: The president skates.

KING: Skates?

O'ROURKE: . . . with absolutely no
punishment whatsoever.

KING: You are—

O'ROURKE: Nothing. No censure. Nothing.
He serves out his term and he gets a great
big book contract and some business deals
and everything's fine except that he blows
up to three hundred pounds and marries a
waitress from Hooters.

KING: This is your— Oh boy.

BOND: We wasted a whole evening to come in
and listen to that?

A week later the Senate acquitted President Clinton on both articles of impeachment. Ten Republicans broke ranks to vote with the Democrats on Article 1 (perjury) while five Republicans voted with Democrats on Article 2 (obstruction). I was having lunch at the Palm in Washington when it happened, and I realized, maybe for just this one moment, the word "bipartisan" had regained definition as Republicans voted with Democrats. But then, maybe, it was still lost by the fact every Democrat voted the party line? I figured it this way: Democrats agreed on something and when you consider the Will Rogers observation that he is not a member of any organized political party because he is a Democrat, there was significance to what had just occurred. I also thought, as did most people, this was an issue the Senate had inherited from the House, so they were just doing their job. And as talk about the vote filtered to my table from the bar in the Palm,

I sipped decaffeinated coffee with skim milk and looked at the caricatures of entertainers and media celebrities and politicians on the wall. "Too bad," I thought to myself, "Jefferson's nowhere to be found. That guy and the other founding fathers were smart enough to decide a president can't be impeached unless there's a two-thirds majority."

Obviously, they must have known about partisan votes back then. It was a good rule; especially when one considers the fact there will always be opposition to the party in power. In the case of throwing a president out of office, a simple majority shouldn't be the deciding factor. As I walked out of the restaurant onto 19th Street, I figured since Jefferson had his own memorial a few miles away, he's ineligible to be on the wall of the Palm.

Linda Tripp was scheduled to come on the show the following Monday, which turned out to be, appropriately enough, Presidents Day. On the afternoon of the interview she stopped by the studio to see the set and sit under the lights for a few minutes. She was concerned about her appearance and I came in to spend a few moments trying to put her at ease. Tripp had been beaten up pretty well in the Leno and Letterman monologues and John Goodman had done a *Saturday Night Live* satire that, to this day, kills me (and to show how well I can read an audience, I didn't bring it up while talking with Linda). That night she came on the set with new hair and a new look. And in between every segment, she would ask either the crew or me, "Am I doing okay?" She was nervous, but she knew she had to do this and she did fine.

KING: You think you changed this country?

TRIPP: Oh heavens.

KING: Are you saying then, this presidency?
Do you think—

TRIPP: No, I mean, look, I'm sorry. I think he
tarnished the presidency. I believe the
country, at least, realizes that much, that his
behavior tarnished the presidency. It will
recover and I don't flatter myself that I had
anything to do with that. But certainly, here
on Presidents Day, think of the legacy that
leaves.

I had asked Tripp about taping Monica Lewinsky because
a lot of people, myself included, wondered how you can be
a friend to someone and at the same time record conversations without their knowledge. Tripp was facing a criminal
proceeding in Maryland for doing just that but couldn't use
the word "taping" without incriminating herself. So right
there on the air we had to come up with a different word.
Tripp suggested "documentation." This was like a flashback
to the campaign where I interview a candidate who refuses
to say he or she is a candidate when the entire reason they
are on with me is that they are a candidate. So, in the same
spirit, the State of Maryland obviously accepted the idea that
documentation wasn't taping. What the heck, we had just
gone through a year where oral sex wasn't sex so this wasn't
really that big a deal. Tripp said she taped Lewinsky to protect herself from a perjury charge were she asked to testify
about knowledge of Clinton's relationships with other women.

Whatever words are used, twenty years from now, to describe these times, I know historians will watch CNN tapes
to make the choice. There, they will find how we struggled
with technology. Events moved faster. History, which I used

to think of in terms of years and decades, is now measured in minutes. I was the guy who slept through history classes at Lafayette High School because I got tired of listening to a teacher tell me what the Spanish-American War meant fifty years after it happened. Now, I was wide awake trying to understand the meaning of the past twenty-four hours.

One word that will be seen and heard a lot is "boggled." Almost as soon as Bill Clinton was acquitted and a sense of closure was at hand, word started to spread about what direction the Clintons will go after they leave the White House (hey, we were already talking about who was going to move in, so this makes perfect sense to me). But the story that was starting to have legs was Hillary Clinton would run for the Senate seat being vacated by New York's Daniel Moynihan. And I wasn't the only one to use that word when I brought on *Washington Post* vice president at large Ben Bradlee, Hugh Downs of ABC, Christian Coalition President Pat Robertson, and *U.S. News & World Report* managing editor David Gergen.

> KING: Ben, let's start with you. What do you
>   make of Hillary Clinton in the Senate?
> BRADLEE: I've given up, Larry. It just boggles
>   my mind.
> KING: Hugh Downs?
> DOWNS: I am like Ben Bradlee. I have no
>   idea . . .
> KING: Pat Robertson, how would you react to
>   a candidacy by the first lady for the office
>   of a senator who is retiring?
> ROBERTSON: I tell you; I don't have a clue.
>   It is mind-boggling.

KING: Mind-boggling. David, they've all said
mind-boggling.

GERGEN: Our minds have been blown out
since a year ago, so we just sort of keep
rolling along. Wonders never cease.

We all were laughing with each answer. The panel was locked at the "mind-boggle" level. I drove home that night thinking something must really be going on in America if all its experts were bewildered. And I rationalized it by saying always having an answer isn't a good thing. Sometimes, you just gotta say "I don't know."

A month later I attended a party for the terrific photographer Annie Leibowitz in the East Room of the White House. I asked Mrs. Clinton about the story and she said "absolutely." The announcement would be formal in early 2000. As it turned out, that's exactly what happened. But it still boggled my mind. And I knew if Eleanor Roosevelt was in the vicinity, she was saying "Do it." I didn't think to ask Arthur Godfrey, though.

Chance Armstrong King entered the world on a warm March night in Los Angeles. His name came from a "chance" meeting a few years earlier when I was in New York City walking out of Tiffany's. I passed a beautiful tall blonde as she walked in. It was one of those moments when I did the should-I-go-back/no-go-to-lunch routine. I went back in. And now I was with Shawn all the way through the procedure, cutting the umbilical cord as Chance was placed on her chest. I looked at them both and could feel tears in my eyes. A father will never know what a mother has to endure during childbirth. It's a moment, though, when every word in any language fails. Shawn later told me she received phone calls from lots of people saying they knew she would do just fine but were concerned about how Larry got through the experience. While standing there looking at our son I knew he was going to be given many things. But what I couldn't offer was any protection from the future. No child is ever given that and, I suppose, it's a good thing. But I wondered what his world was going to be like. And I hoped he wouldn't know his father only from videos of a television show.

Within three weeks of Chance being here, U.S. troops went into Bosnia as part of a nineteen-nation NATO mission. President Clinton addressed the country as the bombing began and Defense Secretary William Cohen did every TV morning news show, two radio networks, PBS's *News-Hour*, *Nightline*, and *Larry King Live*. The frenzy had begun. The daily military briefings started up at the Pentagon while the White House fired up its talking heads division (National Security Advisor Sandy Berger, Secretary of State Madeleine Albright, to name a few) to ensure The Message was delivered about Yugoslavian Prime Minister Slobodan Milosevic being guilty of ethnic cleansing.

On Day 12 of the "Crisis in Kosovo" or, depending on the channel, "Showdown in Bosnia," I had a return visit with Bosnian Prime Minister Haris Silajdzic in Sarajevo (and I might add after the first try at his name, he was still "Mr. Prime Minister" from there on. Some things don't change). He argued for ground troops in the war, which Bill Clinton insisted would not be needed. And then we went to the Yugoslavia chargé d'affaires to the United States, Vladisav Jovanovic, who was in our New York City studio. Jovanovic said the NATO action was "genocidal" and offered the opportunity for any Albanian who had left the country to come home. We went to a commercial break and as I looked at the rundown for the next segment, I could hear Jovanovic in my headset. I looked up and he started talking to me.

"Larry, I want you to know President Milosevic sends his best."

Milosevic? I wasn't following this at all but I said "thank you."

"And he says congratulations on the birth of the child."

Milosevic? The guy being compared to Hitler? I said "thank you." Again.

"He watches your show every day. And Larry?"

I looked up.

"President Milosevic told me to tell you when this is over he looks forward to being back on with you again."

"Thank you," I said while thinking to myself, "again?" By this point we had probably twenty seconds remaining in the break. I got ready for the return but I asked the control room to find out what the hell Jovanovic was talking about. When the show ended, I learned Slobodan Milosevic had been on five years earlier to discuss the Jimmy Carter–brokered cease-fire in Bosnia. I didn't remember the interview at all. Still don't. It kept coming back to history's increased speed. We take an event, look at it from every angle, spit it out, and look for the next event. And when it happens, you miss a lot of what goes past, like conversations with a despot. Sometimes that's good. Sometimes . . .

Shortly after the Bosnia war began I tuned in A&E's *Biography* series and saw a promo for the next night's show: the life of Slobodan Milosevic. Had they aired that show one month earlier, it would have been beaten by the Knitting Channel. I watched it. And as I did, a familiar thought occurred: If you had told me one month ago that I'd choose an interview with the president of Macedonia over Monica Lewinsky, I'd have said you were wacko. Now, I couldn't wait to talk with him.

In late April the topic changed. Fifteen people were dead as a result of two students opening fire at Columbine High School in Littleton, Colorado. The show wasn't just providing information from students and teachers and police who were there; it also offered a place to vent anger and frustration. Later, with guests like Billy Graham, it would become, again, a place for healing. And within an hour of the story, the finger-pointing began. We have always pointed where the blame should be directed but now it was aimed toward the gun lobby for selling weapons like this, at the television and movie industry for making money from violence, at parents for not paying attention to their children, at Bill Clinton for not enforcing existing gun registration laws, and on and on. I'm not copping out here but if this were my call, the finger would be pointed at all of us.

Among the guests that night was a student who knew the two gunmen. CNN had put into effect a rule for this kind of story; anytime a child is interviewed, their parent or guardian has to give consent. I was glad to see other networks and cable operations were doing the same. We were learning as we went along. In the middle of that hour, I was told to go live to our correspondent in Belgrade, Brent Sadler, who was on a satellite phone reporting that massive explosions had just occurred at a nearby government television facility. Three cruise missiles hit the building and the top two floors were engulfed in flames. He handed off to me and I went back to the interview in Littleton. Just as the show was coming to an end I asked one of the guests, defense attorney Gerry Spence, if we were moving toward armed guards in schools.

> Well, you take away all the guns; take away all the
> knives, you still got pipe bombs. You take away all
> the pipe bombs, you still got weapons that kill
> people. So ultimately, we have to take the weapons
> out of the hearts of the people, not out of their
> hands.

I took those words home with me. And as I was driving down Sunset Boulevard listening to the radio report on both the school shooting and about the intense bombing going on in Belgrade, it hit me that I had just talked to a correspondent who described the explosions and never once did I feel anything. People were inside that building but, hell, it was in another part of the world. I worried about becoming numb. Technology can do that. As soon as the front door closed I went to see Shawn, who, I knew, would be holding Chance. And I held on to them both. The little guy hadn't even been here two months and already there was a war going on thousands of miles away and students had died in a school a few states from here. Once again I wondered, and now I worried, just what kind of world was Chance going to face?

When I started reading and hearing and watching stories about George W. Bush raising a million dollars here and another million dollars there while building a campaign war chest of more than $75 million, I also started to dread the 2000 presidential campaign. Still, pundits would come on the show and say this proves how organized the campaign is and it's good they are getting the support lined up early and it shows a wide base will back George W. It was probably all true, but I was fearing a coronation. I wanted a competitive race. He makes for a better show and it attracts people to participate.

The other part of my dread came from the system that was in place to elect the next president. The primaries were front-loaded, meaning if a candidate didn't have enough electoral votes by Super Tuesday, then he or she was out of luck. And it made me wonder about the couple in Montgomery, Alabama, whose primary didn't occur until June. If they wanted someone other than the Super Tuesday victors in either party, they too were out of luck. It didn't seem fair.

The Republicans, however, came from all sides of their aisle to run for president and I was looking forward to some great sessions with each of them. More so, I was hopeful they would be able to reach the disenfranchised voter. There had to be a spark and if that was ever going to happen, this group, which included Pat Buchanan, Alan Keyes, Steve Forbes, John McCain, Gary Bauer, Elizabeth Dole, and Orrin Hatch, was going to deliver. Bill Bradley was campaigning hard to challenge Vice President Gore for the Democratic nomination. And I was starting to think maybe my concern about a coronation was ill-founded.

Late in the year I traveled to, what else, a fund-raiser for George W. Bush in Nashville to do an interview at a place called the Wild Horse Saloon. And we spent the first few minutes talking about why the Rangers just can't beat the Yankees. Bush had a good answer: The Yankees were unified as a team. That's what wins games. Sometimes the simple is the most difficult. Bush had distanced himself from others in his party by calling himself a "compassionate conservative." And it proved to be a good move, especially after the bad press the Republican leadership had been getting for the past few years. That brought us to the last conversation we'd had about the campaign where he admitted to being concerned about its effect on not just him but his family. He had a good answer on that too:

> BUSH: Well, let me put it this way: I understand what a campaign is about. I know it's a marathon. I know it takes incredible patience—
>
> KING: Too long?
>
> BUSH: —and discipline. It's long. You bet it's long. But it's important for candidates to go through the process because it does two things: One, it shows the American people that the candidate's got what it takes to become the president. And it shows the candidate, he or she has got what it takes to be president.
>
> KING: So it should be grueling?
>
> BUSH: Yes, it should be grueling, you need to be scrutinized and questioned.

Bush told me the debates were healthy for the candidates as well as for the public. And by the time I spoke with him, the Republican candidates had already debated once. But Bush didn't participate because of a prior commitment to attend an honorary event for his wife. The excuse didn't fly with the other candidates and it wasn't exactly being accepted by reporters I had spoken with, either. But his overall approach to debates was in direct contrast to that of his father, whom I had interviewed just a few weeks earlier.

> BUSH: To George, the family's important. It's
> everything.
> KING: You would have gone if Barbara were
> being honored and you—
> BUSH: Oh, no question about that.
> KING: No question?
> BUSH: I hated the damn debates anyway.
> KING: But you would have gone?
> BUSH: He did the right thing. I remember
> different debates when I was running at
> different times. Four runs for national
> offices . . . and someone's always telling you
> to do more debates. . . . It's show business.

It was the best interview I had ever done with the former president. He was at peace. And he said, other than the staff, he didn't miss the White House at all. We talked about his years in the Navy in World War II where he served under an admiral named McCain. That's right, Admiral McCain was the father of the man who was now running against Bush's son.

John McCain had already launched his "Straight Talk Express" bus trips in search of voters, which was considered by many reporters to be something new. He made himself available in between campaign stops. The fact was he had done this all along. McCain was always available when I did my late-night radio show to spend a few minutes with me by phone or to sit in the radio booth we had in the Senate and take phone calls on whatever current issue we were talking about that particular day. And he was a frequent guest on the television show as well. I enjoyed having him on because McCain always had nonstop jokes to tell. And nothing was off the record when you talked to him. It went against the norm, which is always the ticket to get noticed. One approach to campaigning was to limit the candidate's exposure, which, in turn, would create an atmosphere of excitement and anticipation when an appearance was made, and provided an opportunity for the other side to define you. But this wasn't McCain's approach—he was always talking. And it was working. Like George W., McCain wasn't allowing himself to be defined by the Republican party.

> KING: Some people say, Senator, your problem
> is that you would do better in a general
> election than in your own party's primary
> because you go against your own party's
> principles often.
> McCAIN: Well, I'm doing very well with
> average Republicans. I don't do very well
> with the inside-the-Beltway crowd and the
> top people in the party . . . but I think I'm
> doing well with average Republicans who
> think they've been disconnected from
> government.

Unlike four years earlier, I was looking forward to the Republican campaign. There was a degree of unknowing, there were blatant differences, and a good national conversation, or depending on the day, argument, was taking place. It also made my job more interesting when an issue could be debated rather than be just another verse in the song sung by the choir.

The same fresh air was to be found with both Al Gore and Bill Bradley. They had agreed to a face-to-face debate in New Hampshire in late October, a full three months before that state's primary. And there were more being scheduled. Gore had proven to everyone he could handle himself in debates. In fact, taking a cue from Barry Goldwater, he suggested Bradley join him on a plane and fly to cities around the country for debates. Gore led in the national polls, but there were problems in New Hampshire. He wanted a chance to change perceptions in the state with the first primary.

> KING: Why would the front-runner challenge the guy who is not the front-runner to debates?
>
> GORE: This is a new campaign. . . . I think the competition will be good for us as candidates and I think it will be good for the country.

Gore told me he was the underdog. It's a Campaign 101 tactic because if you lower expectations, even the most minute success is considered a groundswell. People are more intrigued with the underdog too. Gore was working all the angles.

Years earlier, I had interviewed Bill Bradley for his book *Life on the Run*, which, to this day, is still one of the best sports stories ever written. That's because a good sports story is rarely about what's happening on the field or the floor or the rink. It's about life. And Bradley had spent years as a forward for the New York Knicks. They won the NBA championship in 1970 and 1973. But the story was his experience being a white starting player on a team that traveled around the country. Sports was a small part of that story. And in that first interview it was clear he had aspirations. Let me put it this way: He left the Knicks in 1977 and by 1978 he was a U.S. senator.

One evening Bill Bradley came on the TV show to talk about an issue the Senate was facing, and we had a few moments to shoot the breeze before going on the air. I'll never forget this. He leaned over to me while the crew was setting lights and getting a microphone level saying, "Suppose I answer all the questions tonight like a jock?"

"Bill," I said, "that ain't gonna help your cause here."

He started in. "Well, Larry, you know what they always say, you're only as good as your last election. Well, Larry, I play it one vote at a time. Well, Larry, when you get down to it, it's never just a single senator, it's the whole team that gets the job done." He looked at me and smiled. The crew was in absolute hysterics. "Well, Larry," he started in again, "you know, like I had the vote but you know, I didn't know which way it was, you know, gonna go, so, you know, I said all that work for, you know, all those years, now's the time to make it all, you know, come together." He smiled again and said, "Okay, I'm ready." I didn't know where that came from but Bradley didn't talk like a jock for the rest of the hour.

On New Year's Eve CNN followed the clock across the earth, stopping for just a moment wherever it was midnight. We saw celebrations that used different languages but each used the same word: *wow*. I hadn't heard "wow" for a long time. But a new century is probably as good a time as any to say it. Technology probably is a reason we don't hear the word as often as we used to. Nobody makes plans to attend a World's Fair anymore. We don't need them because television and the Internet are a world's fair of sorts. So maybe that's why "wow" isn't used very often.

I went on the air as the new century began in Rio de Janeiro. People were on the beach cheering and laughing and drinking. And then I went to an entirely different atmosphere. It was Sarnath, India, where 2,500 years earlier, the Buddha began the lesson that we were all part of the same world and what one person does, affects us all. My guest was the Dalai Lama. It was the perfect way to change the calendar even though, for him, this was just another day:

> I think the now modern time, the world becomes
> smaller and smaller. So under these circumstances, I
> believe the concept of "we" and "they" as something
> independent, completely separate, that concept I
> think, gone. So whole world is just like one entity.

As I listened to the not-so-perfect English, the Dalai Lama's words made more sense than most of the words I'd heard all century. I had a job where I could talk with presidents and despots and victims and entertainers. And if the actions of one person can affect how another feels, then maybe the viewer watching the despot can change the next action, or the president's decision about going to war? Maybe the Buddha had this figured out centuries ago?

All of us had just come through an extraordinary time. And the actions of a president had affected everyone. Technology played a role, both good and bad. But the decisions were still those of a human being. It's always going to be that way. And I was looking forward to saying "wow" a few more times, be it because of a president or a triple play. Best of all, no clicker would be needed.

CHAPTER NINE

Clicker
Shock

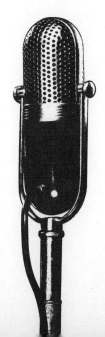

January 2000. The speed of these times has spread from the clock to the calendar. Everyone jokes about one election beginning as soon as another election ends. The thing is, it isn't a joke anymore. In the 1996 presidential election, the Iowa caucus was held on February 12. Four years later it was held in late January. The New Hampshire primary was held on February 20 in 1996 but was bumped up to February 1 in the 2000 campaign. This means the 2004 presidential election will be held in 2003, which makes sense because people will have been campaigning for two years anyway.

Why do we do this? Because we pay attention to the first primary as if it is going to tell us about the second and the third. I don't buy it. Campaigns are bad enough and long enough and the United States ranks low enough in voter turnout among democracies that knowing what happens in

Iowa means something will happen in Wisconsin is not my idea of a good way to increase voter interest. And if Iowa tells us about November, then nobody's gonna watch me interview the candidates in October. So there's a personal thing going on here too.

Iowa is unimportantly important. It carries a lot of weight because it's first but the delegate total to either convention is almost insignificant. And in November Iowa offers only seven electoral votes. Like New Hampshire, Iowa is retail politics. A parade of Republicans and two Democrats told Iowans this year what they wanted to do and then asked Iowans to let them do it. Hands were shaken, the voters were able to look the candidates in the eye, and, in some cases, the candidates sat in the voter's living room to make their case.

But I have never understood the Iowa caucus. Months of campaigning and millions of dollars are spent here for a meeting that begins at 7:00 P.M. with a result predicted by the networks at 7:01 P.M. And in the days leading up to this event, reporters and producers bitch about the snow while whispering what someone else is saying about such and such a candidate. I hear the same lines every time I get to town. "Did you hear about Keyes saying he's thinking about saying such and such" or "I'm told Forbes will make a surprise stop at this or that diner and buy lunch for everyone." Only the names change. Still, it works better this way than if the candidates were decided only by states with huge electoral votes. And that raises the question: Does this first test of the voter say anything about the future? Yes.

Well, sometimes.

Iowa has the reputation of being, for the most part, anything but a way of forecasting, unless you view a defeat in the caucus as a hint of good things to come. Now it doesn't always work that way: Jimmy Carter won Iowa in 1976 and ended up with the job he wanted. But in 1980, George Bush beat Ronald Reagan in the Iowa caucus. By November, he had another job but it wasn't the one he originally wanted. Four years later, just to prove there are no absolutes, the Reagan-Bush team took Iowa. In 1988, Bob Dole beat George Bush in Iowa. Bush won the GOP caucus in 1992 while, who else, Bill Clinton came in fourth on the Democratic side. In 1996, Bob Dole won the Republican race in Iowa, but did so by only three percentage points over Pat Buchanan. But George "Dubya" Bush took the state by the largest margin on record (41 percent of the vote), and he was feeling pretty good when he talked to me minutes after winning the caucus:

> BUSH: I'm extremely happy. Not only am I
> happy, I'm thrilled. This is a huge victory
> and it's a victory of message and organization.

Although it was a convincing win, I still saw the race as competitive. Steve Forbes and Alan Keyes, who finished second and third respectively, had almost as many votes combined. And John McCain, who was considered Bush's real competition, hadn't even shown up to campaign in the state and still got 5 percent. On that cold night in Des Moines, I asked Jeff Greenfield if this had any significance because I sure didn't know what was happening:

> GREENFIELD: The history of spin is that
> candidates very rarely come on and say, I'm
> a little upset with what happened tonight,

especially when they won. But what I am
saying is, I think there is a small, but
palpable danger ahead for George W. Bush,
other than the fact that John McCain is
leading in New Hampshire.

Bush continued to call himself a "compassionate conservative" and filed paperwork to trademark the words so that
no other candidate would try to jump on the bandwagon. As
this happened, Warren Beatty, who was giving thought to
making a run himself, said he would trademark the word "liberal." And as that happened, the Democratic National Committee filed its paperwork to do the same with the phrase
"fiscally conservative but socially moderate." You know, things
like this just ruin a guy's day. I woke up that morning and
the first thing I said to Shawn was, "Gee, I got this feeling
of being fiscally conservative . . ." It was proof the world "has
gone mad today—" which may be copyrighted by Cole Porter,
now that I think about it. I should look into owning the
words "I don't know," since I use them all the time.

My read of the phrase "compassionate conservative" (all
note: This is owned by George W. Bush, so what I'm going
to do here is just borrow it for one second but he gets all
the credit) is that it's Bush's attempt to attract voters turned
off by the far right wing of the party. And after the events
of the past two years, deserved or not, it was a good move.
So when we talked about his definition of the compassionate conservative theme, this led to the abortion question,
since that, among other issues like honor, family, trust, and
the Second Amendment, occupied the framework of conservative values. Bush stayed on their side:

KING: Isn't a fetus a product of a rape or a
product of incest still a living thing?

BUSH: Well, as you know that if the country
ever were to come to be voting on a
constitutional amendment, then I would
support the exceptions. I understand that
we've got a long way to go there. And so
the next president must herald life and
explain the value of life to the American
people. And that's what I intend to do.

KING: But you would favor the exceptions.

BUSH: I would favor the exceptions.

This was something I just didn't understand. And on the
night of the Iowa caucus when we were more concerned with
vote totals than another abortion debate, this wasn't the moment to get into it. But if a person believes abortion is killing
an unborn human being, trying to gradually slide into the
three exceptions (a fetus that is the result of rape or incest
or threatens the life of the mother) doesn't change the fact
it is still a human being. To me, it's either one side of the
street or the other. I'm not arguing for or against abortion,
I'm just questioning the rationale that is used here. I've hosted
hundreds of debates on radio and TV and at conferences on
this issue, and I'm not certain if anyone has ever changed
their mind as a result of the forums. It's decided inside rather
than in all the arguments outside.

While campaigning in New Hampshire, John McCain
was asked about abortion too. But the question had a familiar ring (read: Dan Quayle and Larry) because he had to answer what he'd do if his fifteen-year-old daughter became
pregnant. McCain said it would be a family decision and not

his daughter's alone. Bush got the same question about his twin daughters and said it's personal. It proved that a person can talk forcefully in public about this key issue, but when it becomes a family issue, there will be discussions about whose decision it ultimately becomes and what that decision will be.

We had assembled a panel for the Iowa counting that included former Texas Governor Ann Richards, who had become a "former" as a result of losing to George W., and Jack Kemp, who had run with Bob Dole four years earlier. As soon as I finished talking with Bush about abortion, Richards and Kemp started in:

> RICHARDS: It is being brought by the guys who are running against him in his own party. And it's a tar baby he can't turn loose of.
> KEMP: You know, with all due respect, will he be dogged by the left, the pro-abortion folks? Yes, absolutely.
> KING: No, she's saying he'll be dogged by the right.
> RICHARDS: I certainly hope so in the general election.
> KEMP: Oh no, I disagree with that. He has clearly put himself on the side of that Reagan plank that was in the '80 platform. He may get dogged by both the left and the right.

Bush was taking the position that any attempt to pass a constitutional amendment banning abortion would be defeated in the Senate. He was right on the money. And so he decided to slowly make the case why *Roe v. Wade* had to be overturned and, if a constitutional amendment went before the states, he would support the exceptions. The problem, however, was that the issue wasn't going to be handled at his preferred pace. It never is, regardless of who's running. But this already volatile topic was even more volatile because most believed the next president would select as many as four Supreme Court justices. And that could change the balance from no change in *Roe v. Wade* to overturning the 1973 decision.

The pundits had been right about Al Gore beating Bill Bradley. Still, it was a weird feeling to spend so much time talking about what might happen, or how something else could happen, or why it worked that way, and then have the hard facts appear in front of you. Bradley went down by a 2–1 margin. I always feel the air going out when possibilities become impossibilities. But if Bill Bradley felt the same way, he sure wasn't giving any indication of plans to make an exit. Besides, we still hadn't decided, even with the pundits at work twenty-four hours a day, if Iowa was a test.

For me, the news on the night of the Iowa caucus took place far from Des Moines. As the votes were being counted, I learned that Democratic strategist Bob Squier was dead at age sixty-five of colon cancer. We ended the show that night with a clip of an interview I had done with him six years earlier. He said this was a different time for politics and part of the reason was there were so many news outlets trying to find "the new in the news." I looked around the Iowa set we were on, thought about the electronic town halls we were a part of, the questions being asked, and, of course, the speed at which it was all happening. Bob was talking about the year 2000 in 1994. Things were moving faster than I thought.

Non–electronic town halls, though, was how John McCain

had been campaigning throughout New Hampshire. When I spoke with him on the night of the Iowa caucus, he had appeared at more than a hundred of these forums (and when it was over he would have attended 114). Since it is a pundit's job, and to a lesser extent an interviewer's, to connect the dots between events in the hope there might actually be some sort of cause and effect, I asked McCain to look ahead.

> McCAIN: I see it very close. I see a large undecided, as always. I think some citizens in New Hampshire will change their mind three or four times between now and a week from tomorrow . . . I think the outcome is going to be very close.
>
> KING: Will Iowa affect New Hampshire?
>
> McCAIN: Well, history shows that it doesn't. But I— I think I'd have to leave that to other pundits.

McCain was right. I was starting to hear more and more that voters focus very late on a candidate. I left Iowa with a single thought: In these accelerated times where history is three minutes ago and Tuesday is speeded up to Monday, maybe important decisions like who should be president are still handled with reflection and deliberation? I sure hope so.

IOWA CAUCUS 2000

George Bush	41%	Al Gore	63%
Steve Forbes	30%	Bill Bradley	35%
Alan Keyes	13%		
Gary Bauer	9%		
John McCain	5%		

TURNOUT:
1996 IOWA CAUCUS: 200,000
2000 IOWA CAUCUS: 150,000

When historians write the story of the 2000 presidential campaign (the first version will be completed just as the California polls close on election day), much of it will be about the debates, which is how we measure a candidate, but the focus will be on the number of debates between candidates. Less than twenty-four hours after we had results in Iowa, both Democrats and Republicans gathered in New Hampshire to address issues and each other. CNN carried it and, of course, we talked about it. Two things happened in the separate encounters: George Bush played it safe and Bill Bradley didn't go after attacks from Al Gore about the cost of Bradley's health care proposal.

I kept thinking of Michael Dukakis. In 1988 the Massachusetts governor was campaigning against George Bush and was slow to answer charges about prison reform and liberalism. He later admitted to me, in a conversation off the air, it should have been handled differently:

> It was clear that by '92, no Democratic candidate
> would attempt to blow off the attack stuff. I mean, I
> tried to do that and, obviously, it was a huge mistake.
> Clinton was ready from the get-go. He had a unit in
> his campaign of ten people called "the defense
> department" and all they did was be ready for the
> attacks and respond.

I suppose we'd like to think of the perfect campaign between candidates as resembling something like William F.

Buckley's *Firing Line* where voices aren't raised and issues are argued without one-liners. It ain't gonna happen. On the night of the debate, historian Michael Beschloss made the point we may all look back on this, including Bill Bradley, and say Bradley's chance to topple the incumbent vice president was to go into this campaign with both fists. He didn't do it. Given another chance, I still don't think he'd do it.

In sports, it has now become common for a coach to be interviewed along the sidelines during halftime and players interviewed immediately after a game. In political coverage, we do the same thing, which proves there are few original ideas in this business. I went right to Bill Bradley after the panel discussion and asked about what we *hadn't seen* in the debate with Al Gore:

> So the question is, what kind of politics do we want?
> Do we want a politics that holds people to higher
> standards, or do we want a politics where we just sort
> of spiral to the bottom and everybody attacks
> everybody?

I appreciated Bradley's insistence to take the high road, which, of course, is a diplomatic way of saying I didn't understand why he wouldn't go negative. It is a lofty idea, but when the day is over—and we're talking politics here—the high road is usually a dead end. Bradley also said in that segment that he thought he had done a good job with counterpunches. I'm no expert but I didn't see any being thrown by the senator. He gave the "spiral to the bottom" answer a lot. That's because he was asked about it a lot.

A week later the entire country was focused on New

Hampshire to get a sense of how the candidates were going to be received in the first primary and, of course, if this would be a sample of things to come (every president has won New Hampshire except, guess who, in 1992?). Exit polls all day were showing strong support for John McCain. And that was the buzz throughout the hotel as, again, producers and correspondents started in again with the banter about what they had heard from somebody inside one of the campaigns. Like Iowa, it seemed I was hearing the same things but with different names. McCain was going to go to a VFW post and Gary Bauer was going to a church somewhere and Bill Bradley was going to shoot hoops with a local high school basketball team and on and on and on. I was interested in the primary but I just didn't care about all the "might-be/could-be/won't be" going on. And, of course, I listened to it all. High roads don't work in campaigns and they don't always work in coverage of campaigns, either.

By 4:00 P.M. we knew what was going to happen as a result of exit polling. I've never been polled after casting a ballot but, obviously, the people of New Hampshire are truthful when they answer the questions. If asked, I'd say I voted for Hitler. Guess that means I can't live in New Hampshire.

The story was John McCain. He had beaten George W. Bush by a double-digit margin. Again, there was excitement as all the nonstop supposition we'd had for weeks was tossed and replaced with cold facts. After congratulating McCain, and before getting on a plane for the flight to South Carolina where the next primary was to be held, George W. Bush spent a few minutes with me on the air.

BUSH: I will tell you this—I am—he came at
me from the left here in New Hampshire,

and so it's going to be a clear race between
a more moderate-to-liberal candidate versus
a conservative candidate in the state of
South Carolina.

KING: Are you shocked tonight, Governor?

BUSH: No, I am not shocked at all. I am a
realist and realize that sometimes there's
bumps on the road to the White House and
the state of New Hampshire oftentimes is
that bump in the road.

I could see what was going on here. New Hampshire
was over. Bush was talking to the conservative South Carolina Republicans and framing John McCain as the more
liberal of the two choices. My show was being used to deliver the message. I knew it. Bush knew it. What nobody
knew was whether or not South Carolina Republicans
knew it.

Al Gore slid past Bill Bradley in New Hampshire. That
was the news: slid. Since their last debate a week earlier,
Bradley had gone so far as to say Al Gore was lying. But that
was the limit of his "new politics," as he called it, which, in
another life, had been called the high road. Gore responded
to the close vote by saying he had become a better candidate. Through the evening I wondered, albeit to myself, if
we were dealing with the fact that Gore had won or that
Bradley had lost. I leaned toward the latter. And I asked our
resident pundit Jeff Greenfield how he saw the New Hampshire result:

Unless Bradley has a message to deliver to core
Democrats, as we get down into these next primaries

on March 7, he's in trouble, despite the fact that he
did recover and made a strong showing tonight.

Was New Hampshire a test of the future? Absolutely.
Bradley never got "on message." That was a phrase people
started using a lot. If you were going to do well, you had to
stay "on message." Shoptalk was creeping into our jargon and
it isn't surprising, I suppose, when so many of the talking
heads had an earlier life running campaigns. It was Bob Woodward, however, who offered the idea that Bradley ought to
stay in the race just to make Gore improve with every primary. And it was the first hint I'd had of a possible Gore-
Bradley ticket. The panel that night in New Hampshire
started laughing. I did too. And all the while I was thinking, you know, this makes sense.

NEW HAMPSHIRE PRIMARY, 2000

John McCain	49%	Al Gore	52%
George W. Bush	31%	Bill Bradley	47%
Steve Forbes	13%		
Alan Keyes	6%		

And then there was New York. How many lines have
been written and uttered and even just thought about The
Way Things Are, but then, there's New York? The world
works like this, but then, there's New York. It makes sense
here, but then, there's New York.

All eyes were on the Senate race for the seat of Daniel
Patrick Moynihan, which was becoming a battle between
New York City mayor Rudolph Giuliani and Hillary Clinton. The first lady made a formal announcement that she
was a candidate in early February. Nobody will remember her

speech, nobody will remember the issues she would go after. Nobody will even recall if it was made in the city or upstate (it was upstate and that's my final answer). Instead, they remember the song. And the controversy. I spoke with political observer Bill Maher about the ramifications.

> MAHER: She's going on stage to make the
> announcement. They put a tape of Billy
> Joel, probably his greatest hits. The song
> "Captain Jack" plays.
>
> KING: I know the song.
>
> MAHER: I love that song. And it talks about
> drugs and masturbation and liquor. He
> [Giuliani] says because that song is playing
> when she got on stage that she's saying yes
> to drugs and masturbation. And that's
> ridiculous.

But this was New York. Innocence is always suspect. I asked Giuliani about when he was going to make an announcement and he looked at me like I was crazy. He told me there were no plans to make an announcement. If anything, he was just going to file some paperwork in July. See, there's a way to do it and there's New York.

> KING: You can't run a normal campaign, can
> you, against someone like that? Don't you
> say, "Isn't this going to be weird?"
>
> GIULIANI: No.
>
> KING: No?
>
> GIULIANI: I mean, everything's weird in New
> York.

I figured it this way: On election day New Yorkers will go to the polls to pick a United States senator. If there's a presidential race of some kind going on, they might vote in that too. But there wasn't any pundit anywhere who could have predicted how weird the New York senate race was about to become.

I had been asked to moderate a debate to be seen around the world among the three remaining Republican candidates in South Carolina. CNN aired it from Seawell's Banquet Center in Columbia in front of a live audience. George W. arrived in South Carolina for an eighteen-day campaign calling himself "the reformer with results." McCain, who was using campaign finance reform as a theme, said his win in New Hampshire proved the Republican party had recovered its heritage of reform. I was starting to worry that someone was going to trademark that word.

More important, I was looking forward to this opportunity because so many of the other debates seemed to get bogged down with goofy rules about thirty seconds for a response and questions that went on forever. Debates are the best format we have to learn the differences of ideas but if the format gets in the way, what happens to the idea? I wanted to try something different and that was to do what I've been doing for the past thirty years: control the ninety minutes myself rather than by a format.

Alan Keyes was waiting offstage when I arrived. I have always liked the former assistant ambassador to the United Nations (he worked with Jeane Kirkpatrick), but with only single-digits showing in the New Hampshire primary, I didn't think he belonged in the debate. He was eloquent, he was smart, he certainly was conservative and it was clear he

257

wasn't going to be president. And you know what? Those are crumby reasons to keep someone out of the national discussion. But I'd have preferred the duet of Bush and McCain because the differences wouldn't be watered down by a third voice with no chance of winning.

Keyes and I said hello and engaged in the usual how's-it-going banter until George W. showed up. We spent a minute or two talking about, what else, baseball. And then McCain appeared. He didn't seem himself. He seemed off. Not even a joke. Not even the same joke. The room turned cold. These guys didn't like each other.

Bush nodded. "John."

McCain looked at him. "George."

There was an uncomfortable quiet moment and then Bush said, "Hey man, it's politics."

McCain glared back. "There is more to life than politics."

And that was the moment we were called on stage to spend an hour and a half learning the differences. We covered China and the World Trade Organization, rogue states and terrorism, concerns about the U.S. military being overdeployed and undertrained, abortion, tax cuts, the death penalty, and, of course, the campaign. McCain had run an ad comparing George W. Bush to Bill Clinton on the issue of trust. Bush had held an event in which a veteran said McCain had turned his back on those who had fought in wars. Bush waited until the next day to say he didn't think that was the case (McCain had spent five years in a North Vietnamese prison camp). Bush had spoken at Bob Jones University, which bans interracial dating and calls Catholicism a cult and never suggested these policies were out of line. Bush charged that McCain's people had labeled the Christian Coalition as "bigots." Despite every claim of running a positive campaign, both Mc-

Cain and Bush were running ads that proved it was anything but positive. And this was the only moment of the debate that I thought Alan Keyes had something to offer.

> KEYES: We have a school system that needs to
> be put back in the hands of parents and all
> I'm sitting here listening to is these two
> guys go on about their ads.
> BUSH: He asked about it and—
> McCAIN: . . . we're running nothing but a
> positive campaign from now on. . . . I hope
> George—
> KEYES: It seems to me, let their ad people go
> into a back room and fight it out and let
> the American people hear what they've got
> to hear about the issues.

We had two commercial breaks and neither McCain or Bush said a word to each other. Even the debate I moderated between Dianne Feinstein and Michael Huffington in 1994 was warmer than this one. When it was over, I was happy with the job I had done. Indeed, we had gone through the you-said/no-I-didn't routine in regard to ads but we had also covered a lot of real territory too.

The visit Bush made to Bob Jones University seemed innocent enough to me at first. Ronald Reagan had gone there. So had Bush's father and Bob Dole and Jack Kemp. I disagreed with the rule that a black and white or Hispanic and an Asian couldn't date and I thought the labeling of Catholicism as a cult was, well, out there with the wacko element, but I thought the decision to speak at Bob Jones was a good one. Issues like this bring me back to the feeling we don't learn anything when we don't talk to one another. And if George Bush had said "no thanks" to Bob Jones and gone somewhere else to campaign that day in February, we'd have never heard much about the rules at the university. My interest wasn't in changing what I thought to be a completely insane view of the world in the name of Christ (and this wouldn't be the first time that ever happened) as much as it was trying to understand how they could view the world this way.

Bob Jones himself had appeared on my late-night radio program ten years earlier when the university lost its tax-exempt status in a Supreme Court ruling regarding private schools and social issues; in this case, interracial dating as well. We spent a few hours going through the reasons and taking calls from around the country. And when the issue came up after the Bush speech, Jones called me asking for an hour to make his case and talk about the effect the interracial dating controversy was having on the school. He appeared and we talked about it. And he had a surprise:

> JONES: I don't think it's taking it too far, but I
> can tell you this, we don't have to have
> that rule. In fact, as of today, we have
> dropped the rule. We have dropped the rule
> for this reason.
> KING: Today?
> JONES: Today.

That one came out of the blue. Nobody was expecting it. I considered Bob Jones to be one of those people living in the past, hanging on to wrong ideas and not being swayed by either logic or society's will. This decision took a lot of guts and I admired the administration of Bob Jones University for having the ability to decide they were on the wrong side of the issue. After that show, Jones called me to say thank you. I told him he could be proud that the issue had finally been put away and he had done the right thing. I didn't say anything about future candidates for president coming to Bob Jones University, though. Somehow, I think those days are over.

George W. Bush won the South Carolina primary with 60 percent of the Republican vote. It was a win he needed and, as soon as we had the results, talk turned to Michigan and Arizona where primaries were scheduled in less than three days.

SOUTH CAROLINA REPUBLICAN PRIMARY, 2000

George W. Bush:	53%
John McCain:	42%
Alan Keyes:	5%

I was in South Africa on a speaking tour the following week. In question-and-answer sessions everyone wanted to know about John McCain. Half a world away, everyone knew the former POW was the excitement in the campaign. I was asked questions about why George W. and McCain don't like each other and if this might split the Republican party to the point the Democrats can fill in the gap. I was amazed at the perceptive questions and the ability to read the pulse of the United States from so far away. And then I realized, these guys are watching the same programs everyone in the United States watches. CNN is everywhere and that's something I still have to get used to. Distance between most countries is measured only on a map now.

I certainly understood the interest in the Republican battle. McCain was proving he could get in the way of the grand
plan for George W. Bush to be the nominee. This had really
become a lively run for the nomination. The media, whatever that is, had been criticized for being on the side of Mc-
Cain. That was a simplification, which is the MO of media
critics. I was enjoying the competitive race being delivered
by the "Straight Talk Express," because I wanted to see a real
horse race. McCain and Bush were forcing each other to be
better candidates, just as was happening between Bradley and
Gore. McCain and Bradley were the rebels. All of it was
healthy. Like talking to those with whom there are dis-
agreements, challenging the way things are is always a good
check and balance. And we should do it more often than we
do.

The race was not only healthy, it was interesting. Mc-
Cain took Michigan with the help of independent voters,
who could vote in the Republican primary. When I watched
the results I didn't even have the TV clicker in my hand because I wanted to see where this story was going next. It was
a moment that had captured the imagination of the country.
For the Republican party, the issue became "what do we do
now?" For the McCain campaign it was also "what do we do
now?" With a week before the Big Kahuna called Super Tuesday (which every pundit said would result in each party having a nominee) I was sorry to think this was coming to an
end.

Al Gore and Bill Bradley, for the most part, had been
wiped off, to use another favored phrase, "the radar screen."
(I can't link this phrase to any pundit who used to run a
campaign.) They had faced each other at the Apollo Theater in Harlem, which resulted in an exchange of one-liners

about racial profiling. And then they met in a final exchange that seemed totally lackluster. Joe Klein of *The New Yorker* described it on the air as the first debate between candidates *after* the campaign has ended. Another panel member, Tony Blankley, the former press secretary to Newt Gingrich, had another take on why Bradley seemed off his game:

> BLANKLEY: We are contrasting Bradley's performance, the vigor and energy level at Apollo and the other debates, with the energy level tonight. Now something has to explain why it switched. I think most of us think we know what it is, which is that he's pretty much given up making a fight out of it.

In fact, after that debate the discussion moved on to who Al Gore was going to select as his vice president. That was the moment I knew we had come to the end of Bill Bradley.

On Super Tuesday, one third of all the delegates needed for the party nomination were selected. In fact, 39 percent of the electorate had a chance to go to the polls. Never before has there been such a Super on a Tuesday. And it was a romp. Gore won in a shutout, Bush took nine states including two caucuses and McCain won four in New England. To borrow a line my radio friend Don Imus uses twenty-seven times every hour (and he hasn't copyrighted this as far as I know), "it's over." In fact, it was so "over," that within half an hour of the program that night, we started in again with possible Bush and Gore selections for vice president. I remember this evening because each pan-

elist (Bill Bennett, Bob Woodward, Dee Dee Myers, and
Former Senator George Mitchell) began their observations
with the words "anything is possible." Even though the
evening was a romp, in these times of "anything is possible" or "anything goes," the job of a pundit becomes all the
more difficult.

When Bradley came on to congratulate the vice president, I had the feeling he would call it a game right there.
Yeah, you guessed it. Larry was wrong. The panel started dis-
secting why Bradley's "new politics," as he called it, was a
nonstarter. Bob Woodward said there had always been a distance between the candidate and the voter. The expectation
was he would go one way (endorse Gore) and the reality was
he didn't.

> WOODWARD: It's almost as if he thought he
> was playing basketball, that somehow if
> people could have him, if they knew he was
> going to move left and shoot right, they'd
> be able to block the shot.
> KING: He was in a zone, and he wants to stay
> in that zone.

I walked away from Super Tuesday thinking about the
next eight months. There would be two conventions and
there would be debates, and certainly, there would be lengthy
discussions about vice presidents. If the experience of the last
few months was any indication of things to come, Bush and
Gore were going to show their differences by attacking rather
than having an intellectual discussion. They had learned their
lessons from political combat. We'd still hear complaints

about negative ads but we'd watch them. It made me wonder if there might be another way.

I imagined future candidates would have something like a "Gore Channel." One could use their TV clicker and see the candidate live, maybe even have a conversation with the candidate while sitting in their own home, find out positions the candidate has on abortion (that issue ain't going away), learn where they will appear next for a debate, and, no doubt, watch their opponent be defined as a part of the Establishment-Politics-As-Usual Club.

Maybe someday campaigns will seek out independent voters with ads on shows like *Larry King Live* aimed directly at them. The ad would be a presidential candidate calling the viewer by name and saying what a schmuck his or her opponent is while asking for a donation. Maybe we really could vote from our homes via the Internet, and maybe it will take place over a weekend rather than on a Tuesday in the middle of a workweek? Maybe there will be another third party candidate who will shake up the other two?

I decided all of that is just one crazy idea after another, resulting from being tired after a long day. But as I said that to myself, I realized we are living in a time when crazy ideas have a way of becoming real.

SUPER TUESDAY, 2000

Number of state primaries: 11

Number of state caucuses: 5

Total delegates: 1,315 Democrat (2,170 needed to nominate)

                605 Republican (1,034 needed to nominate)

Al Gore: 859 delegates   George W. Bush: 552 delegates

Bill Bradley: 324 delegates   John McCain: 106 delegates

Alan Keyes: 0

LARRY KING

Number of states with record turnout in GOP primary: 6

Number of states with lower voter turnout in GOP primary: 2

Number of debates: Republicans: 13

Democrats: 9

Source: *Federal Election Commission*
Committee for the Study of the American Electorate

CHAPTER TEN

Too Much and Not Enough

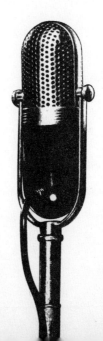

May 2000, Los Angeles. Having some experience with political campaigns, dating back to smacking Senator John F. Kennedy's car in Palm Beach two years before he announced for president, I don't give anybody an argument when the topic turns to "these things go on too long." But then you have to ask questions (which I have been known to do from time to time), like what is too long and how much is too much? And every time I've done this there is a long moment as the wheels turn in search of the answer. "Too long" and "too much" are accurate descriptions, but where do you go after making the point? The answer is, I have absolutely no idea and neither does anybody else.

All of this was going through my head after we knew George Bush and Al Gore were the nominees eight months before the election. If you asked them, and I did, what do you do until the conventions, the answer is "work hard, get the message out, talk with real Americans, and put in place a party of inclusion, not exclusion." All of this is lofty and good, but between Super Tuesday and the October debates, I don't think a lot of people are paying a lot of attention to the next president of the United States. And when you have stories about a six-year-old child plucked from the Atlantic Ocean after his mother drowns trying to get him out of Cuba, well, there aren't even a lot of people paying attention to the current president of the United States.

Look at it this way: My wife, Shawn, was about to give birth to our second son, Cannon, and the time from conception to delivery was shorter than the time from the New Hampshire primary to election day. So it takes longer to campaign for the most powerful job in the world than it does to bring a child into the world. When I mentioned this fact to Shawn, who at the time was in her eighth month, she made it clear real fast that if anything is too much and too long, it sure isn't the length of a presidential campaign. It was, to be diplomatic here, a brief conversation.

On one hand, with 500 channels and the Internet available, you would think a candidate could get the word out about vision and issues and differences from others seeking the same job quicker than the way it was with only three networks and PBS. On the other hand, with 500 channels and nonstop news cycles and polling and the Internet, there is an information overload. So every time I would hear people say there was too much coverage of the Bush-Gore race using talking heads and pollsters and pundits, I had to ask, "Well, would you prefer there be not enough coverage?" And then we start all over again as to where "not enough" ends and "too much" begins. Besides, even though we were eight months out from election day, both Gore and Bush were trying to appeal to the independent voter. I was fascinated by it. And, despite the little boy named Elian, I knew I was in the minority.

Of course, we could make rules, such as the campaign begins on a particular day and no sooner. And of course, if we did that, within two minutes of the rule going on the books, every candidate (and unannounced candidate) would be out there months or maybe years prior to the start date on a "listening tour" or "fact-finding mission" while raising a million dollars with a coffee klatch at Sid and Donna Schweitzer's house. The fact of it is, campaigns go on too long. I've never interviewed a guest who has said, "You know, Larry, I wish I could spend more money as a candidate" or "You know, Larry, I'm here to announce I'm in for the 2008 election." We've been talking about campaign finance reform for years and as we do, the Republicans raise $19 million on the same evening that Democrats raise $26 million. Now that can be called "right" or it can be called "wrong." But everyone also agrees you can't make a rule saying only $794.67 can be raised per evening for a candidate. Too long and too much and too expensive are too much a part of these times. It happens when anything goes.

In May 1999 we scheduled Al Gore to host *Larry King Live* for one night. It was more than a month before he announced his candidacy and we scheduled an issue-oriented panel, including Oprah Winfrey for the interview. But it didn't happen. E-mails started circulating around CNN about the proposed show from concerned staffers. Republican National Committee Chairman, Jim Nicholson, wrote me a letter expressing concerns about what we were going to do. Me? I thought it was a decent idea. After all, we had already used

Ross Perot, Ann Richards, and Newt Gingrich as substitute hosts. I promoted the show in the nights leading up to the scheduled broadcast. How often does a vice president host a TV show? But the question became, Should a vice president host a TV show when even someone on Pluto knows he's going to run for the White House? CNN gave up on the plan and that night I had to cancel a black-tie event I was supposed to emcee and go to work. I understood the concern and I backed the decision, but on a personal level, the issue seemed much ado about nothing. I was asked about it at lunch and dinner for weeks afterward and every time I said the same thing, "Folks, it's a talk show. It ain't rocket science. It ain't gonna change the November election, which, last time I looked, was still more than eighteen months away." There is nothing wrong with the vice president of the United States hosting one night. Had CNN said Al Gore or Bill Bradley or George W. Bush or John McCain could host a week's worth of shows, then an argument could be made for a candidate (or noncandidate) having an unfair advantage. But it never was suggested. I saw the entire episode as one more example of journalism becoming too involved in its own self-importance.

But it also brought up the how-much-is-too-much question (and this was happening more and more). If one night of Al Gore is okay but five nights of Al Gore isn't, then where is the line of demarcation? Is it two nights or is it one and a half? Should each candidate appear in the same week or should this only occur on Thursdays so they aren't up against *Survivor*? I didn't have the answer. Nobody did. I'll lay odds nobody ever will. To this day I will tell you the whole argument was about air: You couldn't see where too much began or where an okay ended.

And a year later it happened again, but this time, it was about credentials. For Earth Day, ABC brought actor Leonardo DiCaprio (who was absolutely fantastic in *What's Eating Gilbert Grape*) to the White House for an interview about environmental issues with President Clinton. All hell broke lose. What is *an actor* going to ask the president of the United States? How many softball questions are going to come out of this? There are many capable reporters who would love to sit down with Bill Clinton and ask questions and, instead, the White House agrees to a lightweight Q and A session with a pretty face. I kept thinking to myself, "Wait a second. Are people who have a White House credential the only people who can ask questions? DiCaprio cares about these issues." There was jealousy going on here. It reminded me of my own experience eight years earlier when critics were complaining about candidates going on *Larry King Live* instead of sitting down with Dan Rather or a White House correspondent. There was a perception of self-importance in 1992 and it continued to exist on Earth Day, 2000. It was ridiculous then and it's ridiculous now and when it happens in the next five years, it'll still be ridiculous. And I'll lay odds future presidents will sit down with Main Street America as well as celebrities and answer questions about a variety of issues. Now if future presidents *only* sit down with actors to answer questions, then there is a legitimate concern. And while we've probably had some presidents whose elevators didn't reach the top floor in the past, on this issue I don't think there will be a president who would be dumb enough to do something like that. Oh boy, there goes another prediction . . .

*   *   *

These times of "too much" and "not enough" aren't limited to politics. On Thanksgiving Day, 1999, CNN and other news operations carried a story about six-year-old Elian Gonzales being rescued from shark-infested waters by two fishermen. His mother and twelve others had left Cuba three days earlier in a sixteen-foot motorboat seeking a better life in the United States. They didn't make it. The boat sank and Elian was the only survivor. It was a great news story. He was a good-looking kid, he had come from Castro's Cuba, and was settled in Miami's highly charged Cuban community with his great uncle Lazaro Gonzalez. Elian was a story. And as happens from time to time, the story became a story. The frenzy had returned.

My ability to predict continued to score at the zero level. A few days after Thanksgiving, for instance, I announced to Shawn we were doing another Elian story that night, but I fully expected the kid to be reunited with his father, Juan Miguel Gonzalez, and probably go back to Cuba, and hearing a lot of argument about whether relations with that country should be established. I saw the Elian story as a ten-minute Judge Judy. We had an orphaned kid, his father in a foreign land, and some relatives in Miami who didn't want the father to have anything to do with the kid. Both sides will be heard while Elian recuperates in the hospital and that's it. Next case.

But I had lived in Miami and should have known better. I knew the people who had been sent to the United States as children for a better life while their parents or relatives stayed behind in Cuba. It was an emotional issue as much as it was a political issue. And that's always a tinderbox. And even though anyone with a pulse was saying (1) let's keep Elian's best interests in mind and (2) the Elian story has gone on too long, the six-year-old was seized by FBI agents in Miami and flown to Washington to be reunited with his father. Cameras had been set up outside and inside his great uncle's home. Everyone kept saying "too much" and as they said it everyone was watching. I asked Dan Rather about it on the air one night and the seasoned CBS anchor told me he agreed it was too much. Then he looked at me and said, "But we're sure not going to shut down our camera."

After the fifth month of the story, I started thinking Elian might attend the University of Maryland and both Castro and Clinton would be at the graduation. The words "Miami relatives" took on a new meaning, even for a Jew from Brooklyn. I figured his talkative cousin, Marisleysis, will be the weather girl on a Miami TV station. I mentioned this during lunch a few times and the table would start laughing. But then there was a moment when everyone would become silent, and someone would always say, "you know, Larry, it's possible." This is the thing about these times: You make a joke or you intentionally say something that is out there, and then you have to think if it really is out there or, just maybe, right next to you.

I'll put it this way: If you had told me twenty years ago we would be making airline reservations on a computer from our home or writing electronic mail to people on the other side of the country, that the Cold War would be over while Castro was *still* in power, that cars would have satellite maps on the dashboard, that people would be buying dot-com companies in droves and not have a clue what the dot-com company does, and that the president of the United States would have an affair with an intern, tell us he didn't inhale when asked about smoking dope, lie directly to the American people and yet possibly win a third term if he were allowed to run, I'd have said you're a looney tune. So maybe Elian will be a future Ambassador to the United States from Cuba or a United States Ambassador to Cuba? Folks, it really isn't out there at all. The significance of the Elian story is that we will begin talking to Cuba and traveling to Cuba. And, somehow, this just doesn't seem so extraordinary when compared to what has happened in the past twenty years.

CNN had scheduled me to do a face-to-face interview with Nelson Mandela in our New York studio, which meant after the television show was over in Los Angeles I was going to spend the night on the red-eye flying across the country. I stopped at home to say goodbye to Shawn and Chance before heading out to LAX. When Chance was carried into the living room by our nanny, Becky, she told him, "Say goodbye to Daddy." Chance looked at me and then looked at the television. He waved to the TV. Daddy was the man in the box, not the man in the living room. I flew across America that night wondering if I should be concerned about how a fourteen-month-old child sees the world and his dad. And I wondered at what point does a child see the difference between the man in the box and the man in front of him? I'll be honest. It bugged me.

I got my answer a few weeks later. In early June ads began in fifteen states at a cost of millions of dollars outlining reasons why the Democrats have good ideas. And as soon as they hit the airwaves, the Republican National Committee began running ads outlining reasons why they have good ideas. In both cases, soft money was being used to suggest one side is ready for the job. In both cases, Americans were being asked to consider these ideas, maybe even let them sit for a while and then, on their own, connect the dots linking them to either George W. Bush or Al Gore. Our perceptions of both candidates were being shaped in part by these spots. Later, after the conventions, the ads would become more aggressive. But for the time being, the ideas of what kind of world we could have if one of these men becomes president was there in the box. Besides a quick TV appearance at a campaign stop shown on the TV or heard on the radio or reported in the morning paper, our general perspective of Al Gore and George W. Bush was limited, even though the political junkie had more than enough information available on the Internet. Like Daddy, the man in the box wasn't the man in the living room. Unlike Daddy, television had become a significant way for the electorate to learn what this person was all about. And unlike Chance, hopefully those watching television could understand what they see in a sixty-second political ad doesn't necessarily reflect who the candidate is or what the candidate stands for. That's why there are talk shows. And that's why the viewer has to be smarter, or maybe more dubious, than ever before about what is on the screen.

Which is why we have debates. And why in an interview on *Larry King Live*, Vice President Gore made an offer he knew George W. Bush would refuse:

> GORE: Eliminate the thirty-second and sixty-
> second TV and radio ad and, instead,
> debate twice a week with a different issue
> each time. Would you be willing to host
> one of the first debates, Larry?
> KING: Absolutely, of course.

> GORE: Well, I accept. Now . . . this is in
> Governor Bush's hands. He and his party
> can decide to accept this or they can start
> the ad war. And I hope they make the right
> decision because it is very much a sincere
> offer.

After Gore's segment was complete we went to a commercial break. I was feeling pretty good about the chance to be involved again in the debates when one of the panelists told me Gore had just been on the *NewsHour* with Jim Lehrer and had made the *same* offer to Bush as well as to Lehrer to host. I had one thought as the floor director counted me out of the commercial: This was typical Al Gore. I bought it and I wasn't even watching television. And people told me, after watching that show, Gore didn't play well in their living room.

A few days later George W. Bush was on to talk about his just concluded bury-the-hatchet meeting with John Mc-Cain. I knew, from personal experience, these guys didn't like each other. But for the sake of unity in the Republican party, it was absolutely essential these two candidates appear together and for John McCain to say he supported George W. Bush. They did just that and McCain said what he had to say and as he did, it was a perfect Body Language 101 example of words not matching heart. That night on the show Bush gave me another nugget that cemented my suspicions:

> BUSH: We had a good, frank discussion on
> campaign funding reform. And I really
> appreciate his friendship and appreciate his
> endorsement as well.

KING: I remember being with both of you in
South Carolina and the mood was rather
tense and that's sometimes hard to get over
with.

BUSH: . . . You're right. In South Carolina
there were some tense moments but after all
we were in the middle of a debate.

One thing I have learned in the more than forty years
of interviewing people is, if they tell you they had a "frank"
discussion with someone, it is usually code for a yelling match
with clenched fists and a few adjectives. Newt Gingrich used
to come on the show and talk about having "frank" conversations with Bill Clinton just as Tip O'Neill would talk to
me about his "frank" conversations with Ronald Reagan. Now
I wasn't in the room when Bush and McCain talked, but if
I were a betting man, I'd say it's a mortal lock they both
wished they were someplace else even though they both had
to be there.

I asked Bush about Gore's offer to stop the ads and start
the debates. He said if he believed Al Gore was sincere, he
might consider it. But he didn't believe it. And while he
wanted to debate, Bush said it was too early to start. "There's
an old tradition in American politics," he told me, "you have
to have the debate on the debate." I thought about the years
since that night driving to my new job at a Miami radio station and listening to the Kennedy-Nixon debate. I didn't recall any debate before a debate but I'm certain it was there.
I'm certain Lincoln and Douglas debated the debate. And
while every campaign for president has one side challenging
the other side to debate early, nobody can tell you who made
the challenge by election night. And after all the pundits

I've talked to in the ten elections since 1960 with Kennedy and Nixon, nobody has ever told me one guy won because he started the debate about debates earlier than usual. This says something about what the image of the man in the box appears to be, and after the debates and the final swing through the country, what the man really is. The truth is, even though anything goes, we really still can tell the difference.

And then there was New York. I was at home in Los Angeles and, of course, the clicker was in my hand. And there was Rudolph Giuliani on TV saying he had prostate cancer and was dropping out of the race against Hillary Clinton. And as I heard the words "this is not the right time for me to run for office," I thought back a few months earlier to the show I did with the New York mayor when he said he wasn't even going to announce he was running for the Senate. But now, Giuliani had to announce he wasn't a candidate, and in addition to prostate cancer, his marriage was over. You couldn't have written this as a script. But then, people had been saying that throughout the Clinton-Lewinsky story.

I interviewed New York Governor George Pataki that evening, who had been in conversations with Giuliani earlier that day about the pending announcement. He told me he wasn't going to get into the Senate race even though many in his party were urging him to do just that. Pataki said he liked being governor. And since there happened to be a presidential campaign going on as well, I asked the next question:

KING: But if offered the vice presidency with Governor Bush, you would accept?

PATAKI: Larry, now you're getting into
    hypotheticals, and quite simply I want to
    see Governor Bush become President Bush.
    I'm going to do everything I can to help
    him win that race.

The Veep question has always been part of every presidential election. Today, it shows up earlier and it is asked nonstop, and while I will continue to ask it, and variations on a theme of the next VP, I will never expect an answer.

A week before the Republican convention in Philadelphia, I sat down with George W. Bush for an interview about his campaign, his acceptance speech, and, of course, his choice for vice president. I knew former Defense Secretary Dick Cheney had been heading the search committee and I knew the short list of candidates was getting shorter as the convention start grew closer. Off camera, Bush guaranteed I would have the first interview with his Veep selection. Never, did I expect it was going to be Cheney, although his experience and knowledge in foreign affairs was going to complement the Bush campaign. And when his name was announced, I thought back twelve years to the Republican Convention in New Orleans. Cheney was a Wyoming Congressman and a former Chief of Staff to President Ford. And having just survived a third heart attack, he was scheduled to leave the convention after George Bush received the nomination to undergo a bypass operation. He knew I had gone through it eight months earlier and cornered me in a stairwell of the Superdome asking to see my scars and tell him what to expect. I held nothing back and Cheney never flinched. This was a tough guy. And when we sat down together, Cheney and I spent a few moments talking about diet and medication before we got into issues pertaining to the job for which he was about to begin campaigning. Had you asked, I'd have never guessed Cheney.

A few weeks later Democrats gathered in Los Angeles to nominate Al Gore for president. And when pundits weren't talking about how the vice president had to distance himself from Bill Clinton, they were talking about who he was going to select to take the job he'd held for eight years. I had been talking with Norm Ornstein of the American Enterprise Institute who said he'd just gotten off the phone with the Gore campaign and had been told the name was Joe Lieberman. My first thought was "wow, a Jew." And then I thought, "why Lieberman? It sure can't be for Connecticut's electoral votes" But then I thought about Dick Cheney. He was from Wyoming. No electoral vote surges there either. The *Larry King Live* staff had been promised, whomever is the choice, we'd get the first interview and that Gore himself had signed off on the plan. So fourteen hours after the name Joe Lieberman was announced, I was sitting with the Connecticut Senator to introduce him to the world. I thought back to an interview I'd done with his mother earlier that day had and how she'd gone to bed the night before figuring her son wasn't going to be selected. I remembered how a year and a half earlier he had given a speech in the Senate critical of the president's behavior regarding Monica Lewinsky. This, I figured had to be a factor in his selection. Gore was beginning his move away from Bill Clinton. Had you told me where Joe Lieberman would be in August 2000, you'd have been labeled "nuts." Times change. And as these pages prove, change isn't always an easy thing to do, much less understand.

*   *   *

A lot has happened since those moments twelve years ago when I sat in a CNN booth at the Omni Arena watching Democrats at work while waiting for the governor of Arkansas to finish his never-ending speech. But some things haven't changed. Bill Clinton still has a tendency to talk too long. We are part of an election that again pits a Southern governor against a sitting vice president. And I remember doing shows on radio and television in 1988 about how much it costs to run for president and how long it takes to do so. Let me tell you something: If the election price tag was too much in 1988, it's beyond too much in 2000.

Politics, however, has become meaner. I can tell you a number of talented people who have a lot to offer in ideas and solutions and who have looked at possibly taking a step into the arena, but then backed away saying "it ain't worth it." And many who have made the step have, later, told me it was beyond what they ever expected it to be. George W. Bush spent a lot of time thinking about this campaign before he ever became a candidate because he had first-hand experience as both a governor and as the son of the president. Al Gore's father was a seven-term congressman and a three-term senator. Gore brings his own congressional experience as well as the vice presidency to this campaign. Both candidates know what they are getting into.

But it's different now. I asked Mario Cuomo what he thought future candidates will face in a run for the White House. He said a few questions have to be asked—and answered—before anything is done relating to a campaign:

> Do I realize in the end this will largely be a
> matter of luck and circumstance whether I
> win or lose? Do I know exactly why I want

this thing? Am I firmly convinced that I
have the answers and the strengths and the
abilities that I know nobody else out there
has? And, am I prepared for the scrutiny?

Cuomo isn't sure the pendulum will swing back and, as of this moment, isn't optimistic about the process we use to choose a president. He predicts there will be more questions asked because the media is going to play more of a role. "And that," he says, "creates a questionnaire."

I suppose each of us has some kind of a questionnaire for the person we choose to support for president. That's why we have debates. That's why we watch television talk shows. But we don't want a national questionnaire because if we do, then every candidate will be alike. Every debate will sound the same. Presidents will come from cookie cutters. These times won't allow for that kind of president to be effective.

President Bush's press secretary, Marlin Fitzwater, says the people who want to occupy the White House from now on have to know how to use the media (whatever the media is). It plays more of a role in elections than ever before because there are so many outlets available to candidates . . . and presidents. Roosevelt had America's ear with his fireside chats delivered on radio. And this will be more difficult for a president to do today because the audience is so splintered and sliced and diced. Outside of a nuclear war or a major threat to national security, many of the 500 channels wouldn't think of giving the White House a half hour, much less five minutes. It's weird when you think of all the magazines, newspapers, radio stations, Web sites, and television channels that exist right now and we're talking about the problems a president will have in trying to talk to a sizable population about an important issue. But that's these times.

What both Cuomo and Fitzwater are saying, though, is clear. It is different now. The electorate has more information available, and its attention span is shorter because there seems to be so much more happening than before in any given moment. It's going to be tough for a president to lead when, through no fault of his or her own, people aren't paying attention. This is going to be one of the challenges for those who sit in the Oval Office from now on.

When I am asked to speak to college journalism schools, one question is always posed: Is all of this the result of these times we are in or is all of this the result of technology? I answer by saying we are in a transition. The boundary of when "too much" begins has disappeared. I grew up when there were three networks. Today we have hundreds of satellite-delivered networks, cable, the three original networks, and PBS. And we're trying to learn how to make it all work. The first step, of course, is to put ESPN on the same cable or satellite channel in every city. Once we do that, the rest of this is a piece of cake.

I tell the classes what they already know and, no doubt, what you, the reader, already know: Change is taking place as it always has, but at a pace we've never seen before. There is always a delayed reaction to change because we want to think about it, and then maybe test it, and then, complain about it while yearning for the good old days. And only then, possibly, will we become comfortable enough with change to allow it to make our lives better. Here's what I'm talking about: I don't own a computer. I use an IBM Selectric to type out my USA *Today* column. And I just started using the electric model typewriter a few years ago. Yes, I miss writing it all out on a single sheet of paper and phoning it in. So on a small scale I'm learning the Selectric and I'm trying to get comfortable with remembering to plug it in. The rest of the world is doing the same with the Internet. Bill Clinton talked about change being painful while running for office in 1992. He was right. It is that and more. And Bill Clinton will be the first to say he couldn't have predicted all the changes we've seen since he was sworn in as president.

I hope, one of these days, I can sit down with Chance and Cannon and tell them about the man who was in the White House when they came into the world. He was the most remarkable politician their dad ever saw. He was focused, he never gave up even when many backs were turned against him, and he did good things as well as incredibly stupid things. It is those stupid things that will be the first paragraph of his legacy, because the story of Bill Clinton is the story of an extraordinary person in extraordinary times. That, and having enemies who could self-destruct at just the right moment, is what got him through the tough times. And there were a lot of tough times. I know because I was on the air during all of them. And the viewers of *Larry King Live* learned along with me how (depending on the matter at hand) the pro–Bill Clinton and anti–Bill Clinton forces saw the issues.

I'll tell Chance and Cannon they may never see another person like this in their lives. I know I won't. Most important of all, I hope I'll be able to sit with my boys and talk about these times face-to-face. But if I'm not around, I've made a video talking about these years, this president, and the men who want to be the next president.

I can only hope, if I am on tape, my sons won't have inherited their father's television clicker ability. I hope their times aren't the times when anything goes.

INDEX

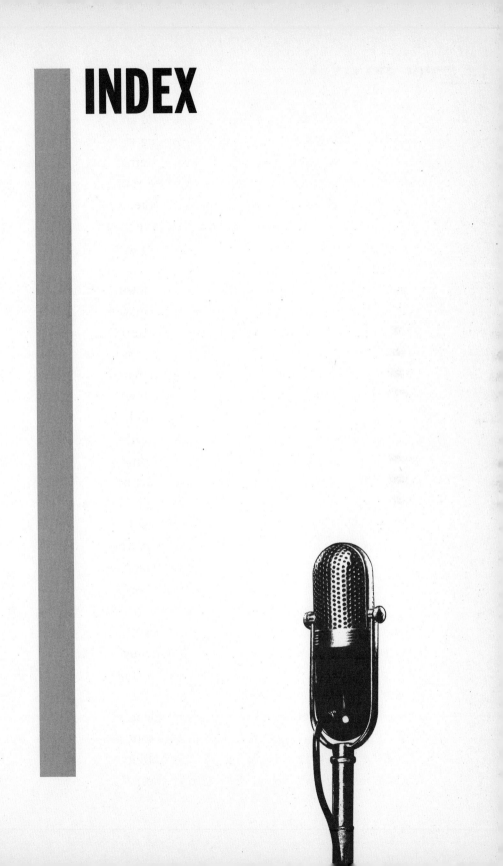